Military Airpower
A Revised Digest of Airpower Opinions and Thoughts

Compiled by

CHARLES M. WESTENHOFF
Colonel, USAF, Retired

Air University Press
Maxwell Air Force Base, Alabama

March 2007

**Muir S. Fairchild Research Information Center
Cataloging Data**

Military airpower : a revised digest of airpower opinions
and thoughts / compiled by Charles M. Westenhoff.

    p. ; cm.

Includes bibliographical references.

ISBN 1-58566-163-5

    1. Air power—Quotations, maxims, etc. 2. Air warfare—
Quotations, maxims, etc. 3. Military art and science—
Quotations, maxims, etc. I. Westenhoff, Charles M.

    358.4—dc22

Disclaimer

Air University Press
131 West Shumacher Avenue
Maxwell AFB, AL 36112-5962
http://aupress.maxwell.af.mil

Contents

Foreword

When Air University Press first published *Military Air Power* early in 1990, the Cold War was ending and US forces were poised to launch Operation Desert Storm. Today's captains and staff sergeants were in grade school. Since then, our Air Force has achieved unprecedented combat successes; enabled great humanitarian efforts; and crossed new thresholds in air, space, and cyberspace. We've added great new chapters to our service's heritage—and our nation's history—and the horizon just keeps unfolding.

The year 2007 marks the 60th anniversary of the US Air Force as an independent service. It's also the centennial of military aviation. In 1907, the Signal Corps established its Aeronautical Division and later released its specification for a "heavier-than-air flying machine." Since then, Airmen have consistently proved themselves as well as the utility of airpower in combat, leaving no doubt that the US Air Force is America's asymmetric advantage. Yet, 2007 also marks the dawn of a new era for the Air Force. Today, America's Airmen are engaged in a dizzying array of worldwide missions that were unthinkable a century ago. Every day Airmen conduct space operations, deliver precision weapons, develop and fly the latest generation of stealth aircraft, move our nation's war fighters and equipment around the globe, fuse advanced sensors with trained analysts to develop exquisite intelligence, conduct aeromedical evacuation of wounded personnel, open and sustain expeditionary bases, operate unmanned aerial vehicles from halfway around the world, and devise and test new war-fighting technologies. And Airmen combine these disparate missions so seamlessly and effectively that it may seem easy. Of course, it is not.

This book is about what Airmen have in common—our heritage, capacity, and future potential. It also illustrates that while we're on the leading edge, we're also part of the sweep of military history. Understanding the way that our predecessors handled their challenges can equip us to better serve our nation. We can learn from both the failures and the successes of soldiers, sailors, marines, and Airmen; the ancient past; and yesterday's headlines.

As military professionals, our interest in learning from others is to gather clues that we can put to work in the future. I encourage you to target your search toward determining how timeless wisdom can be best applied to the optimal use of our armed forces' air, space, and cyberspace power, and to add your own pages to our great story.

T. MICHAEL MOSELEY
General, USAF
Chief of Staff

About the Author

Col Charles M. Westenhoff, US Air Force, retired, is a 1974 graduate of the US Military Academy at West Point. He served two tours as a flight inspection pilot in the T-39 and three tours as a forward air controller (FAC) in the O-2 and A-37. As the chief of FAC Tactics at Nellis AFB, Nevada, he taught at the USAF Weapons School, wrote and edited tactics manuals, and developed precision weapons tactics and procedures. Returning from service as the air attaché in Baghdad, Iraq, during the closing months of the Iran–Iraq War, he served at Air University's Airpower Research Institute. There he led parallel planning for Instant Thunder (the concept plan for the Desert Storm air campaign), compiled the 1990 *Military Air Power* book, and contributed to the 1992 Air Force Manual 1-1, *Basic Aerospace Doctrine of the United States Air Force*. Colonel Westenhoff served as the Air Force Quadrennial Defense Review deputy director in 1996–97 and as commander, Joint Suppression of Enemy Air Defenses Joint Test Force, from 1998 to 2001. Returning to the Air Staff in 2001, he led Red Team planning in support of Operations Enduring Freedom and Iraqi Freedom and served as Checkmate deputy division chief. Colonel Westenhoff served as chief of strategy for Coalition Joint Task Force Seven in Iraq until retiring in 2004. He has served as the senior mentor to Checkmate since retiring. Colonel Westenhoff lives in Reston, Virginia, with his family.

Preface

The number one aim of this book is to supply Airmen with useful thoughts that might help them meet their known responsibilities and the unknown challenges their service will bring. The most capable Airmen are judicious in finding the best material to put into their "clue bags." They continue a long tradition. Nearly three hundred years ago, Frederick the Great searched the best of military thought trying to "acquire perfect knowledge and experience."

The materials in this book are offered as candidates for your clue bag. Some of the quotations were selected for their irony, humor, or incendiary effect. I'm confident that readers will know good sense from nonsense.

This book contains many "old, dead guy" quotations for several reasons. First, they're good. No one has improved on Sun Tzu in 2,500 years. Second, time has graded their work and put them at the head of the class. Third, they wrote clearly.

To identify the sources of quotes, I've used two military principles—brevity and simplicity. Rank abbreviations reflect the official usage of parent services (i.e., Lt Gen for the Air Force, LtGen for the Marine Corps, and LTG for the Army). Those who should be household names are treated as such (e.g., Commanding General of the US Army Air Forces and, later, the first and only General of the Air Force, Henry H. Arnold, is simply Hap Arnold). Also, I have periodically interjected my own thoughts, denoted by italics. Another note, unless other-wise indicated, emphasis in quotes is in the original.

Just as in the 1990 edition, (1) the quota-tions are arranged by subject matter to pres-ent multiple views of each topic; (2) I couldn't include one-tenth of the good material I would have liked to; and (3) any errors are mine.

What's different is the world we live in—and the way it's been shaped by airpower.

CHARLES M. WESTENHOFF
Colonel, USAF, retired
March 2007

Acknowledgments

Gen T. Michael Moseley, chief of staff of the Air Force, had the idea of revising this book. I'm grateful to him for the opportunity to update this work to improve its utility to today's Airmen. The commander of Air University, Lt Gen Stephen "Steve" Lorenz, made this book happen through the able office of the Airpower Research Institute (ARI)—especially Dr. Dan Mortensen and John Conway, as well as the production support of Emily Adams and the Air University Press staff.

On inputs, I had help from the most perceptive of Airmen, including Phil Meilinger, Rob Owen, Lt Gen Dave Deptula, Mace Carpenter, and Bill Andrews. I'm also grateful for the help supplied by the Air Force Doctrine Center (AFDC), spearheaded by Maj James J. Marsh, Maj Ray Fernandez, and Bob Poynor. Both the ARI and AFDC provided sanity checks; Dr. David Mets and Capt Jamie Swisher were very helpful in this regard.

The greatest pleasure of service in the Air Force is the people. We improve from every briefing and debriefing. I've had the honor of flying on the wing of many outstanding flight leads, too many to mention, but will single out two—Gen Chuck Boyd and Maj Gen Chuck Link.

I'm most grateful for the support of a family of avid airpower advocates, and, in particular, I thank my wife, Kelley. Any person who sends you off to a combat zone with cheerful support is worth their weight in gold.

The 1990 book contained 30 pages of material at the end. This included a brief bibliography and biographical snapshots of the sources of the quotations, which did not do them justice. Those wishing to know more about a source can learn as much or little as they wish on the Internet. I do append a list of 20 books that I found most valuable for both editions of this book.

INTRODUCTION

The Challenge

Know and use all the capabilities in your airplane. If you don't, sooner or later, some guy
who does use them all will kick your ass.

Dave "Preacher" Pace
Quoted in Robert L. Shaw, *Fighter Combat*

Every art has its rules and maxims. One
must study them: theory facilitates practice.
The lifetime of one man is not long enough to
enable him to acquire perfect knowledge and
experience. Theory helps to supplement it; it
provides a youth with premature experience
and makes him skillful also through the mistakes of others. In the profession of war the
rules of the art are never violated without
drawing punishment from the enemy, who is
delighted to find us at fault.

Frederick the Great

About Brevity

It would further human knowledge if, instead of writing new books, we would apply ourselves to making decent extracts from those that are already in existence. Then one would hope to avoid wasting his time by reading.

Frederick the Great

> Frederick the Great's writings fill 30 books.

As one veteran Israeli pilot said after the June 1982 air campaign over Lebanon in response to American questions about how much doctrine the Israeli Air Force had written down, "Yes, we have books. But they are very thin."

Barry D. Watts and James O. Hale
Air University Review, 1984

> It is a good thing for an uneducated man to read books of quotations.
>
> Sir Winston Churchill
>
> The checklist is not a substitute for the full text of the flight manual.
>
> Stan Eval "famous aviator"

Regardless of Air Force Specialty Code, we must understand the overall purposes of military air power and then see how our individual duties support those purposes.

> Col Keith W. Geiger
> *Airpower Journal,* Fall 1987

You should understand airpower, and you must preach the doctrine. You will be on staffs where you are going to meet people who do not understand airpower, and you are going to have to educate them. . . . You have got to go out and preach the doctrine of airpower and never give an inch on it.

> Gen Hoyt S. Vandenberg

More than most professions the military is forced to depend upon intelligent interpretation of the past for signposts charting the future.

> Douglas MacArthur

The present state of things is the consequence of the past; and it is natural to enquire into the sources of the good we enjoy and the evils we suffer.

> Ben Jonson ca. 1600

Nothing is comprehensible, except through its history.

> Teilhard de Chardin

Assumptions

A modern, autonomous, and thoroughly trained Air Force in being at all times will not alone be sufficient, but without it there can be no national security.

Gen H. H. "Hap" Arnold

War is a matter of vital importance to the State, the province of life or death, the road to survival or ruin. It is therefore mandatory that it be thoroughly studied.

Sun Tzu

When blows are planned, whoever contrives them with the greatest appreciation of their consequences will have a great advantage.

Frederick the Great

War is not an affair of chance. A great deal of knowledge, study, and meditation is necessary to conduct it well.

Frederick the Great

No study is possible on the battlefield.

Field Marshal Ferdinand Foch

A wise man learns from his experience; a wiser man learns from the experience of others.

Confucius

There is only one method of fitting our intellects to be ready for war, and that is by studying the history of air warfare, *and by no means should we neglect naval and land warfare.*

"Squadron Leader"

(*Note:* Squadron Leader was the pen name of the author of *Basic Principles of Air Warfare,* a 1927 classic with the subtitle, *The Influence of Air Power on Sea and Land Strategy.*)

As a nation we were not prepared for World War II. Yes, we won the war, but at a terrific cost in lives, human suffering, and [matériel], and at times the margin was narrow. History alone can reveal how many turning points there were, how many times we were near losing, and how our enemies' mistakes often pulled us through. In the flush of victory, some like to forget these unpalatable truths.

Hap Arnold

Adherence to dogmas has destroyed more armies and cost more battles than anything in war.

Maj Gen J. F. C. Fuller

Many commanding generals spend their time on the day of battle in making their troops march in a straight line, in seeing that they keep their proper distances, in answering questions which their aides de camp come to ask, in sending them hither and thither, and in running about themselves. In short, they try to do everything and, as a result, do nothing. How does this happen? It is because very few men occupy themselves with the higher problems of war. They pass their lives drilling troops and [come to] believe that this is the only branch of the military art. When they arrive at the command of armies they are totally ignorant, and, in default of knowing what should be done, they do only what they know.

Maurice de Saxe

AIRPOWER

AIRPOWER

We have the enemy surrounded. We are dug in and have overwhelming numbers. But enemy airpower is mauling us badly. We will have to withdraw.

> Japanese infantry commander
> Situation report to headquarters, Burma,
> World War II

The gratitude of every home in our island, in our Empire, and indeed throughout the free world, except in the abodes of the guilty, goes out to the British airmen who, undaunted by odds, unwearied in their constant challenge and mortal danger, are turning the tide of world war by their prowess and by their devotion. Never in the field of human conflict was so much owed by so many to so few.

> Winston Churchill

People have preferred to feel rather than know about airpower.

> Common paraphrase of Noble Frankland:
> "People have preferred to feel rather than
> know about strategic bombing," 1963

There are still those who fail to stand back and reflect on the fact that air assets operate in the one medium that surrounds the earth and that touches 100 percent of the earth's population, political capitals, and centers of commerce. Because of the long history of surface warfare and, perhaps, of our very existence on land, air power is not an easy concept to grasp.

Gen Ronald R. Fogleman, USAF, retired, 1997

The United States relies on the Air Force and the Air Force has never decided a war in the history of wars.

Saddam Hussein, 29 August 1990

While Saddam Hussein could rely on like-thinking unsophisticates from his home town of Tikrit to run his army, finding equally doctrinaire individuals who could also fly an airplane was a far more difficult task. (Hitler and Goering had the same problem with the Luftwaffe in the Second World War.)

Richard P. Hallion, 1992

Airpower Theories

There has been a tendency to overemphasize long-range bombardment, and to ignore the versatile application of air power. Our Air Forces were used for any mission considered important, at any given moment. Especially misleading is the distinction made between strategic and tactical air forces. That distinction is not valid in describing the use of air power as a whole, day after day.

Gen Carl A. "Tooey" Spaatz

If we should have to fight, we should be prepared to do so from the neck up instead of from the neck down.

Lt Gen Jimmy Doolittle

Air power is indivisible. If you split it up into compartments, you merely pull it to pieces and destroy its greatest asset—its flexibility.

Field Marshal Bernard Law Montgomery

Air power is like poker. A second-best hand is like none at all—it will cost you dough and win you nothing.

Gen George Kenney

By material, we mean the stuff or goods out of which something is made. Materiel means the finished product, whether it be machine-guns, rivets, photographic film, engines, or bombers. So superior materiel is the key to airpower.

Maj Gen Oliver P. Echols

Air power alone does not guarantee America's security, but I believe it best exploits the nation's greatest asset—our technical skill.

Hoyt S. Vandenberg

The Nature of Airpower

Once the command of the air is obtained by one of the contending armies, the war must become a conflict between a seeing host and one that is blind.

H. G. Wells

In the air are no streets, no channels, no point where one can say of an antagonist, "If he wants to reach my capital he must come by here." In the air all directions lead everywhere.

H. G. Wells

Neither the Army nor the Navy is of any protection, or of very little protection, against aerial raids.

Alexander Graham Bell

The first important difference between air forces and armies is that, within his tactical range, the airman is independent of lines of communication and has no flanks. The only other important difference between armies and air forces is that an air force is not committed to any one course of action.

Air Marshal Sir John C. Slessor

Because of its independence of surface limitations and its superior speed the airplane is the offensive weapon par excellence.

Giulio Douhet

The measure of airpower is the ability of a nation to exploit airspace for its own purposes—and in wartime to deny it to an enemy.

Adm Arthur Radford

Air power can either paralyze the enemy's military action or compel him to devote to the defense of his bases and communications a share of his straitened resources far greater than what we need in the attack.

Winston Churchill

Aerial forces menace all the territory comprised in their radius of action. They can set off from different points and arrive "en masse" on a chosen point. They lend themselves to the offensive because they leave the adversary, until the last moment, in uncertainty as to their objective.

Arsene Vauthier
Paraphrase of Douhet

The air ocean and its endless outer space extension are one and indivisible, and should be controlled by a single homogeneous force.

Alexander P. de Seversky

The very flexibility of air forces makes true cooperation essential. Air forces, at short notice, can be switched from one sort of target to another and, within limits, from one type of operation to a quite different type. There is, therefore, a constant temptation to use them piecemeal to meet an immediate requirement, rather than to use them on a long-term joint plan.

J. C. Slessor

Every soldier generally thinks only as far as the radius of action of his branch of the service and only as quickly as he can move with his weapons.

Luftwaffe general Karl Koller

If we lose the war in the air we lose the war and lose it quickly.

Field Marshal Montgomery

Air Force Airpower

America has only one Air Force. . . . The other Services have aviation arms essential to their specific roles and functions but which also work jointly to project America's air power. . . . It is a potent combination, proven over and over in combat.

GEN Colin Powell, 1993

The soul of an Air Force is range and payload and access.

Gen T. Michael Moseley, 2006

American planners should look at what happened and ask whether these improvisations do not point the way to greater effectiveness. After several decades of insisting that the word service means "parochial," military reformers might ponder the individual merits of the services, each of which can pool a great deal of operational expertise along with a common world view and an esprit de corps difficult to find among a melange of officers.

Eliot A. Cohen, 1994

The other services have air arms—magnificent air arms—but their air arms must fit within their services, each with a fundamentally different focus. So those air arms, when in competition with the primary focus of their services, will often end up on the short end, where the priorities for resources may lead to shortfalls or decisions that are suboptimum. It is therefore important to understand that the core competencies of air and space power are optional for the other services. They can elect to play or not play in that arena. But if the nation is to remain capable and competent in air and space, someone must pay attention across the whole spectrum; that is why there is a U.S. Air Force.

Gen Ronald R. Fogleman, USAF, retired, 1997

While on one hand, soldiers and sailors alike tend to downplay the influence of air power on the modern battlefield, on the other, these very individuals are seen campaigning for further strengthening their service-specific air arms. The problem, it seems, is not with air power, which is acceptable, but with the air force emerging as a rival military service.

Air Commodore Tariq Mahmud Ashraf
Pakistan air force, 2002

An Airman's Perspective

- Land and naval warfare expertise were sufficient, until the invention of the airplane. Operations in the aerospace medium are sufficiently complex and unique to require a new and separate competence. . . . This is the only reasonable and defendable justification for the expense of organizing, training, and equipping an Air Force separate from the Army and the Navy.

- Airpower characteristically moves rapidly and responsively, neither inhibited nor encumbered by mountains, gorges, rivers, or beaches: this isn't doctrine, this is physics!

- Modern airpower's characteristics: Speed, Range, Freedom of Maneuver, and Perspective, give the Joint Force Commander [JFC] freedom of action and a great range of choices.

- It is an airman's job and duty to articulate the ways in which the unique characteristics of airpower can be brought to bear on the JFC's objectives.

    Maj Gen Chuck Link

United States Airpower

Air and space power IS America's asymmetric advantage.

Brig Gen David A. Deptula, 2000

The United States is neither a land nor a sea power, as those terms are usually understood. Other nations have maintained strong air forces, but the United States is the world's first and only aerospace power. We do it uniquely well. But we're also uniquely dependent upon it. Lose command of the skies and space, and the whole thing falls apart.

Philip Gold, 1997

You could give the same airplanes to two different air forces—one of them totalitarian and the other one under a democracy, and the democracy's going to win every time because the air war is about freedom of choice, it's about maneuver, and it's about a regime that's able to entrust a handful of men with a great deal of power.

Maj Gen Chuck Link, 1996

The United States of America is an aerospace nation. Throughout history, great nations have been defined by the nature of their military forces. Certainly, the strength of Rome lay in its legions. . . . England became a world power as a result of the Royal Navy and its ability to control the seas and project power around the globe for that island nation. I think as we move into the twenty-first century, the United States of America will be defined by the fact that it is an aerospace nation.

Gen Ronald R. Fogleman, 1995

It is now an entrenched fact of life that as American air power has become ever more accurate, lethal, and effective, it also has come under ever more intense public attention, scrutiny, and questioning, even as it has, at the same time, heightened not only the nation's political imperatives but also a legal need to be more discriminate in the use of force.

Ben Lambeth

Airpower

The Global
Airpower Perspective

World War II demonstrated for American statesmen and military planners that the world was one seamless strategic problem for the United States.

Eugene M. Emme

Air power is not limited by oceans, by shorelines, by shallow water. It's not limited by mountains or mountain passes or rivers, shallow or deep. It's not limited even by distance.

Gen T. Michael Moseley

The Air Force can deter, deliver a tailored response, or punch hard when required—over great distances—with quick response. We can provide a presence, or put ordnance on a target worldwide in a matter of hours.

Global Reach–Global Power
USAF White Paper, June 1990

In-flight refueling converts the tactical fighter into a strategic, long-range participant. It sustains combat air patrols, enables indirect routing, extends interdiction and strategic penetration depth and increasingly is an integral component of front-line strength.

Air Vice-Marshal Tony Mason
Royal Air Force (RAF)

Link air and space force together. Under the strategic principle that the one who controls outer space can control the Earth, superpowers and military giants are expanding their strength in outer space and the function of [their] air force.

> Maj Gen Zheng Shenxia and
> Senior Col Zhang Changzi
> People's Liberation Army Air Force (PLAAF)

Both Afghanistan and Iraq were air mobility wars. Every single flight into these areas of operation needed some kind of air refueling—fighters, bombers, lifters and even other tankers needed air refueling. Navy carrier-based fighters needed dramatic air refueling to get them the "legs" they needed.

> Gen John W. Handy

The successful execution of the lift portion of Enduring Freedom spotlighted the value of logistics as a weapon system, as well as the fact that effects-based operations entail materiel delivery as well as bombing.

> Ben Lambeth

Space Power

There is something more important than any ultimate weapon. That is the ultimate position—the position of total control over Earth that lies somewhere out in space. That is . . . the distant future, though not so distant as we may have thought. Whoever gains that ultimate position gains control, total control, over the Earth, for the purposes of tyranny or for the service of freedom.

Lyndon B. Johnson, 1958

[As] we showed and proved during DESERT STORM, and proved again during the air campaign over the Balkans, space is an integral part of everything we do to accomplish our mission. Today, the ultimate high ground is space.

Gen Lester P. Lyles

The US must, over the next few years, develop a cadre of experienced, intensely knowledgeable people skilled in applying space to combat. We are talking about an entirely new breed of war fighters, who will ultimately transform the power and scope of warfighting in the same way airpower professionals have done in the last century.

Acting Secretary of the Air Force Peter B. Teets

Space Superiority has to roll off the tongue as easily as Air Superiority.

Gen John P. Jumper

Whereas those who have the capability to control the air, control the land and sea beneath it, so in the future it is likely that those who have the capability to control space will likewise control the earth's surface.

Gen Thomas D. White

Space superiority is our imperative—it requires the same sense of urgency that we place on gaining and maintaining air superiority over enemy airspace in times of conflict. This imperative requires a full understanding of the medium of space, and we will pursue robust space situation awareness leading to space superiority.

Gen Lance Lord

The proverbial first shot of space warfare has already been fired with the advent of jammers designed to defeat the capabilities our airmen derive from space.

Secretary of the Air Force James G. Roche

If you're not in space, you're not in the race.

Gen Lance Lord

Space is a realm in which many military operations are conducted more efficiently than by terrestrial systems. Military satellites have been operating in space for more than twenty years, and our accomplishments in DESERT STORM emphasize that space has unquestionably evolved as a military theater of operations.

Gen Charles A. "Chuck" Horner

In the long haul our safety as a nation may depend upon our achieving space superiority. Several decades from now the important battles may not be sea battles or air battles, but space battles, and we should be spending a certain fraction of our national resources to insure that we do not lag in obtaining space supremacy.

Gen Bernard "Bernie" Schriever

Our space force may need to become a military entity in its own right, equal and apart from our air, land, and maritime forces.

Gen Chuck Horner, 1999

Elements of Airpower

Air power is the total aviation activity—civilian and military, commercial and private, potential as well as existing.

Hap Arnold

The air power of a nation is what it actually has today. That which it has on the drafting board cannot become its air power until five years from now.

Lt Gen Frank M. Andrews, 1937

I have flown in just about everything, with all kinds of pilots in all parts of the world—British, French, Pakistani, Iranian, Japanese, Chinese—and there wasn't a dime's worth of difference between any of them except for one unchanging, certain fact: the best, most skillful pilot had the most experience.

Brig Gen Charles E. "Chuck" Yeager

Why can't they buy just one airplane and take turns flying it?

Calvin Coolidge

A nation may have every other element of air power but still lag behind if its government has no real urge to insure its future development. The attitude and actions of government will fully determine the size of our military air establishment, and greatly affect the efficiency of our civil air establishment, our aeronautical industry and facilities—hence our air power in being.

John C. Cooper

Service aviation must be the spearhead, civil aviation the shaft, of our air effort.

Maj Gen F. H. Sykes, 1922

A large system of commercial aviation will remain an abiding support for the national aircraft industry and will at the same time provide those reserves of personnel which are essential for the expansion of aerial strength in case of need.

P. R. C. Groves

There aren't a lot of movies made about airlifters. There's no "12 O'Clock High" or "Top Gun" about those heavy aircraft, but, despite their lack of glamour, they are arguably the most potent tool this nation has for shaping the international arena.

Secretary of the Air Force Sheila E. Widnall

It is this beat, this precise rhythmical cadence, which determines the success of an airlift. This steady rhythm, constant as the jungle drums, became the trademark of the Berlin Airlift, or any airlift I have operated.

Lt Gen William H. Tunner

We have learned and must not forget that, from now on, air transport is an essential of airpower, in fact, of all national power.

Hap Arnold

The interesting thing is that now you will never hear about airpower separately from space power. When the Air Force talks about what it brings to the [joint] fight, the first thing is air and space power. The bottom line is, everything on the battlefield is at risk without air and space superiority.

Gen Thomas S. Moorman Jr.

Expeditionary Airpower

When the United States forces first landed in North Africa, there were nine airdromes that our planes could use. Within a few months there were a hundred. Mud, and later dust, were the worst problems. With the Axis on the run, airfields were built even faster. One request was received to build several airfields in the Sbeitla sector; seventy-two hours later, all were in use.

Hap Arnold

We move on time lines that simply will not work if we have to wait for support for our expeditionary forces.

Gen Ronald R. Fogleman

Allied Force remains the most accurate air campaign in history, but it was a logistics masterpiece that orchestrated the opening and operation of 20 bare bases and the bed-down and maintenance of more than 1,000 US and allied fighters, bombers, support and reconnaissance aircraft, and helicopters.

Secretary of the Air Force F. Whitten Peters

The aim of a military organization is not to make do with the smallest number of supporting troops but to produce the greatest possible fighting power. If, for any given campaign, this aim can only be achieved by having a hundred men pump fuel, drive trucks, and construct railways behind each combatant, then 100:1 is the optimum ratio.

Martin van Creveld

Agile combat support reaches outside of pure logistics. It includes functions like force protection, Red Horse engineers, services, contingency medical care and other combat support functions.

Gen Ronald R. Fogleman

A recipient of a PGM [precision-guided munition] does not know or care if the weapon came from near or far, or from what kind of platform, or from what kind of base.

Brig Gen David A. Deptula, 2001

No soldier can fight unless he is properly fed on beef and beer.

John Churchill, First Duke of Marlborough

Teamwork allows us to be an effective fighting force—a rapid expeditionary force capable of deploying anywhere in the world in a minimum of time and in austere conditions—not operating from where we are stationed, but from where we are needed, not when we can, but when we must.

Gen Michael Ryan

Diplomacy will not be strengthened by a military force and a deployment structure that give an opponent time to raise questions about the true extent of U.S. power and influence, especially when those questions start to resonate in the United States.

> Dr. David A. Kay
> United Nations chief nuclear
> weapons inspector, 1998

"Complete" Uses of Airpower

What gave American air power such predominance in the Gulf, and what makes the United States incomparable as a military power, is its systemic quality.

Eliot A. Cohen, 1995

There was no line of cleavage between strategic and tactical air forces. It was over-all effort, uniting all types of aircraft, coordinated for maximum impact.

Tooey Spaatz

The four principles of air power that I set out were:

1. To obtain mastery of the air, and to keep it, which means continually fighting for it.

2. To destroy the enemy's means of production and his communications by strategic bombing.

3. To maintain the battle without any interference by the enemy.

4. To prevent the enemy [from] being able to maintain the battle.

Air Marshal Hugh Trenchard

Once real mastery of the air was obtained, all sorts of enterprises would become easy. All kinds of aeroplanes could come into play.

Winston Churchill

The single clear lesson of World War II was that the visionaries were correct that all future warfare would be dominated from the air. They agreed on that. What they argued about was just how airpower would dominate surface warfare.

David MacIsaac

Objectives of
Airpower Employment

To avoid the fate of the vanquished is an ob-
ligation of statecraft second only to the sol-
emn duty of controlling war itself. Whatever
the future may hold, victory in war now rides
on the wings of the fighter and the bomber,
and air power is essential to national survival. But the only ultimate security lies in
the conquest of war itself.

Edward Meade Earle

Objectives vary considerably in war, and the
choice of them depends chiefly upon the aim
sought, whether the command of the air,
paralyzing the enemy's army and navy, or
shattering the morale of civilians behind the
lines. This choice may therefore be guided by
a great many considerations—military, political, social, and psychological.

Giulio Douhet

Air power will play the leading role in our response to the security challenges of the un-
charted future. It will in some circumstances
be the only engaging form of military power
and in others the form upon which successful surface operations depend.

Lt Gen Charles G. Boyd, 1991

The air campaign may be the primary or supporting effort in a theater.

Col John A. Warden III
The Air Campaign

Economic and
Political Objectives

The real importance of Munich . . . is that it was the first victory for air power—no less significant for being temporarily bloodless.

J. C. Slessor

The Berlin Airlift was the first real event of the Cold War. Many people in high places thought it was the first event in World War III.

Gen T. Ross Milton

The Strategic Theory postulates that air attack on internal enemy vitals can so deplete specific industrial and economic resources, and on occasion the will to resist, as to make a continued resistance by the enemy impossible. . . . It is conceivable that there will always be one industry, such as the oil industry in Germany, so necessary to all phases of the national war-making ability that its destruction would be fatal to the nation.

Hap Arnold

The flexibility which the range of aircraft gives to air forces permits concentrated effort against a particular target system or complex without need for concentration against a particular target of the system; hence the enemy is unable to keep his defenses in one geo-graphical area.

Air University (AU) Manual 1, *United States Air Force Basic Doctrine*, 1951

Strategic air assault is wasted if it is dissipated piecemeal in sporadic attacks between which the enemy has an opportunity to readjust defenses or recuperate.

Hap Arnold

The advocates of all-out air-power maintain that area destruction and mass annihilation can effectively destroy the war potential of the adversary and lower his strength and will to continue the struggle. It should be remembered, however, that the objective of war is the exercise of effective control over the political elite of the state to enforce a political decision.

S. T. Das

It is easy to say, as many people do, that England should isolate herself from Europe, but we have to remember that the history of our insularity has ended, because with the advent of the aeroplane, we are no more an island. It does not matter whether we like [it] or not, we are indissolubly tied to Europe.

Stanley Baldwin

Psychological Effects

The constant arrival of wounded, without any battle taking place, makes us all think. The conduct of operations is such that the Panzer Divisions are being decimated by naval gunfire and low flying aircraft without being able to fight. It can't go on like this anymore! In such a situation, one can calculate the day on which the division will finally be annihilated.

SS Brigadefuhrer Kurt Meyer

Air power is, above all, a psychological weapon—and only short-sighted soldiers, too battle-minded, underrate the importance of psychological factors in war.

B. H. Liddell Hart

Not only our military reverses but also the severe drop in the German people's morale, neither of which can now be overlooked, are primarily due to the unrestricted enemy air superiority.

Joseph Goebbels, diary, 15 March 1945

The internal situation in the Reich is governed almost exclusively by the air war. Here is our real weakness in the overall conduct of the war.

Goebbels, diary, 17 March 1945

It is not so much the existence of a military establishment that determines a people's will to resist as it is their confidence in it, as witness the collapse of Japan while still armed with effective ground forces numbering over three million. In other words, the will of a nation to resist is not always dependent on armed strength, but rather upon its belief in its chances for political success.

Maj Gen Dale O. Smith

It is improbable that any terrorization of the civil population which could be achieved by air attack would compel the Government of a great nation to surrender. In our own case, we have seen the combative spirit of the people roused, and not quelled, by the German air raids. Therefore, our air offensive should consistently be directed at striking the bases and communications upon whose structure the fighting power of his armies and fleets of the sea and air depends.

Winston Churchill, 1917

Control of the Air

Without a reasonable degree of air superiority, no air force can effectively assist land or sea forces or strike at the enemy's war potential.

Arthur William, Lord Tedder

There are no silver medals in the air superiority event. You either win it or you get your ass kicked. When you get your ass kicked in the air, your people are getting their ass kicked on the ground.

Maj Gen Chuck Link, 1996

The only real security upon which our military principles can rely is that you must be master of your own air.

Winston Churchill

Air superiority is not the God-given right of Americans. It doesn't just happen. It takes a lot of people working hard to produce the capabilities that provide it for U.S. forces.

Gen Ronald R. Fogleman

The minimal requirement for a successful [maritime] operation is a favourable air situation. Air superiority will be a requirement for sea control where a robust challenge from the air is possible. Air supremacy is a necessary precondition of command of the sea.

Royal Navy, *The Fundamentals of British Maritime Doctrine*, BR 1806, 1995

Air control can be established by superiority in numbers, by better employment, by better equipment, or by a combination of these factors.

Tooey Spaatz

After all, the great defence against aerial menace is to attack the enemy's aircraft as near as possible to their point of departure.

Winston Churchill
Memorandum, 5 September 1914

The first and absolute requirement of strategic air power in this war was control of the air in order to carry out sustained operations without prohibitive losses.

Tooey Spaatz

One general inference to be drawn has been that in twentieth-century war, defeat will almost always be avoided (and outright victory likely gained) by the side that has secured air superiority. Indeed, a more comprehensive perusal would probably show that virtually the only exceptions concern counterinsurgency warfare.

Neville Brown

The future battle on the ground will be preceded by battle in the air. This will determine which of the contestants has to suffer operational and tactical disadvantages and be forced throughout the battle into adopting compromise solutions.

Field Marshal Erwin Rommel

To use a fighter as a fighter-bomber when the strength of the fighter arm is inadequate to achieve air superiority is putting the cart before the horse.

Adolf Galland

The Ardennes battle drives home the lesson that a large-scale offensive by massed armor has no hope of success against an enemy who enjoys supreme command of the air.

Maj Gen F. W. von Mellenthin

On 15 December [1911] an aircraft was hit by anti-aircraft artillery shrapnel. The pilot then swooped low over the gun battery, as if to congratulate the gun crew, and dropped some of his visiting cards as he flew by. This precedent was unlikely to be followed in subsequent conflicts.

Air Vice-Marshal Tony Mason

The Gulf War was the first rather large-scale regional war in which the number of aircraft destroyed in beyond-the-horizon air combat exceeded those destroyed in visual air combat. It indicates that beyond-the-horizon air combat technology is maturing.

Col Ming Zengfu, PLAAF, 1995

Airpower and Maneuver

What I hope we're beginning to understand is airpower's ability to destroy enemy forces without giving the enemy as much to shoot at.

> Maj Gen Chuck Link, 1997

We are seeing right now an historic evolution in maneuver warfare: to the interdependent fight, where long-duration mass on the ground can be exchanged for rapid massing of resources of awareness, of detection, and of instant communications to deliver concentrated and precision strike.

> Secretary of the Air Force Michael Wynne

The attention of commentators usually focused on the violent application of air power, but in fact, its nonlethal characteristics were no less important. For example, airlift delivered over half a million tons of dry cargo to the Gulf region. It also made possible such movements as the repositioning of the Eighteenth Airborne Corps for the left hook into southern Iraq and Kuwait. That repositioning took C-130 aircraft landing every seven minutes for thirteen days, moving fourteen thousand personnel and over nine thousand tons of equipment over four hundred miles.

> Eliot A. Cohen, 1995

The primary objective of Allied forces in the Southwest Pacific is to advance our own network of air bases deep into the Japanese perimeter.

Hap Arnold

Movement is the essence of strategy. This is true even though strategy is not confined to the military art: the implementation of every political decision requires movement. It may be messages that move, or men, or money, or munitions.

Stephen B. Jones

Air strategy begins with airplane ranges. Airplane ranges determine the location of bases. The proximity to the target of the bases under one's control fixes the weight and rhythm of the attack.

Tooey Spaatz

The Americans, with minimum losses, attacked and seized a relatively weak area, constructed airfields, and then proceeded to cut the supply lines to troops in that area. The Japanese Army preferred direct assault, after German fashion, but the Americans flowed into our weaker points and submerged us, just as water seeks the weakest entry to sink a ship. We respected this type of strategy for its brilliance because it gained the most while losing the least.

Lt Col Matsuichi Iino
Japanese Eighth Area Army

Strange as it may seem, the Air Force, except in the air, is the least mobile of all the Services. A squadron can reach its destination in a few hours, but its establishment, depots, fuel, spare parts, and workshops take many weeks, and even months, to develop.

Winston Churchill

We do not have to be out and out disciples of Douhet to be persuaded of the great significance of air forces for a future war, and to go on from there to explore how success in the air could be exploited for ground warfare, which would in turn consolidate the aerial victory.

Maj Gen Heinz Guderian, 1937

The fact of British air superiority threw to the winds all the tactical rules which we had hitherto applied with such success. In every battle to come the strength of the Anglo-American air force was to be the deciding factor.

Field Marshal Erwin Rommel, 1942

Utilization of the Anglo-American air forces is the modern type of warfare, turning the flank not from the side but from above.

Vice Adm Friedrich Ruge
Rommel's naval aide at Normandy

Somebody has to be on the ground. I don't want them to have to fight their way in. I want the American soldier to only have to worry about mud on his boots, not blood. At the end of the day, the American soldier's best friend is the American airman. But only if we get our story told.

Maj Gen Chuck Link, 1995

Only through speedy delivery of combat forces to favorable positions can decisive impact be exerted. Among various delivery measures, air transport is the most effective action because of its strong mobility, fast speed, and less restrictive geographic conditions.

Maj Gen Zheng Shenxia and
Senior Col Zhang Changzi, PLAAF, 1996

Interdiction, Attrition, and Counterland

It is infrequently claimed that the maintenance of a favorable situation in the air is the *principal* task of both bombers and fighters in the field. This is definitely not so. Air superiority is only a means to an end. The object of air superiority is the control of air communications, *firstly for our own use* and secondly to deny it to the enemy. And the use we require is to "conduct operations against an enemy"; and this, in a land campaign, means to *break down* the resistance of the enemy army.

J. C. Slessor

The greatest secret of war and the masterpiece of a skillful general is to starve his enemy.

Frederick the Great

When one army is full and another starving, lead and steel are hardly needed to decide the victory.

Sir John Fortescue

The idea that superior air power can in some way be a substitute for hard slogging and professional skill on the ground is beguiling but illusory. Air support can be of immense value to an army; it may sometimes be its salvation. But armies can fight—and not only defensively—in the face of almost total air superiority.

J. C. Slessor

For our air offensive to attain its full effect, it is necessary that our ground offensive should be of a character to throw the greatest possible strain upon the enemy's communications.

Winston Churchill, 1917

There is a great difference in the mental attitude of aerial crews when "close-in" Army targets are attacked as opposed to the normal strategical target. Crews will fly through intense flak to a "close-in" target and do an excellent piece of work. Ten days later the same crews will fly into just as intense flak to attack a bridge or supply dump and do only a fair job. In spite of the losses and injuries sustained to date in Air-Ground cooperation work, morale always reaches a new high during such periods of operation.

United States Army Air Forces
42d Bomb Wing report, World War II

Air interdiction and ground maneuver must be synchronized so that each complements and reinforces the other. Synchronization is important because it can create a dilemma for the enemy that has no satisfactory answer. His dilemma is this: if he attempts to counter ground maneuver by moving rapidly, he exposes himself to unacceptable losses from air interdiction; yet if he employs measures that are effective at reducing losses caused by air interdiction, he then cannot maneuver fast enough to counter the ground component of the campaign.

Price T. Bingham

If the enemy has air supremacy and makes full use of it, then one's own command is forced to suffer the following limitations and disadvantages:

- By using his strategic air force, the enemy can strangle one's supplies, especially if they have to be carried across the sea.

- The enemy can wage the battle of attrition from the air.

- Intensive exploitation by the enemy of his air superiority gives rise to far-reaching tactical limitations for one's own command.

Erwin Rommel

The argument has been advanced that the Air Force should be concerned with land objectives, and the Navy with objectives on and over the water. That distinction is to deny the peculiar quality of the air medium, the third dimension. The air is indivisible; it covers land and sea.

Tooey Spaatz

Airpower has become predominant, both as a deterrent to war, and—in the eventuality of war—as the devastating force to destroy an enemy's potential and fatally undermine his will to wage war.

GEN Omar Bradley

As the aeroplane is the most mobile weapon we possess, it is destined to become the dominant offensive arm of the future.

J. F. C. Fuller

70 percent of casualties and injuries to enemy troops in the Vietnam War were caused by U.S. air firepower. Half the Arab tanks damaged during the fourth Middle East War were destroyed by the Israeli Air Force. During the Falkland Islands war between Britain and Argentina, 90 percent of the 29 vessels that were lost were due to air strikes. All the above indicates that with the rapid development of air weapons, the focus of modern war is gradually shifting to the air. Air firepower is becoming the backbone of joint military forces.

Maj Gen Zheng Shenxia and
Senior Col Zhang Changzi, PLAAF, 1996

Airpower Prophecy

I dipt into the future far as human eye could
    see,
Saw the vision of the world, and all the
    wonders that would be;
Saw the heavens fill with commerce,
    argosies of magic sails,
Pilots of the purple twilight, dropping down
    with costly bales;
Heard the heavens fill with shouting, and
    there rain'd a ghastly dew
From the nations' airy navies grappling in
    the central blue.

> Alfred, Lord Tennyson
> "Locksley Hall," 1842

Heavier-than-air flying machines are impossible.

> William Thomson, Lord Kelvin
> President, Royal Society, 1895

An uninterrupted navigable ocean that comes
to the threshold of every man's door ought
not to be neglected as a source of human
gratification and advantage.

> Sir George Cayley (1773–1857)

The example of the bird does not prove that
men can fly. Imagine the proud possessor of
the aeroplane darting through the air at a
speed of several hundred feet per second. It

is the speed alone that sustains him. How is he ever going to stop?

Simon Newcomb
Independent, 22 October 1903

In order to assure an adequate national defense, it is necessary—*and sufficient*—to be in a position in case of war to conquer the command of the air.

Giulio Douhet

The bomber will always get through.

Stanley Baldwin

Engines of war have long since reached their limits, and I see no further hope of any improvement in the art.

Sextus Julius Frontinus
Strategemata, Introduction to Book III, AD 84

Few people who know the work of Langley, Lilienthal, Pilcher, Maxim and Chanute but will be inclined to believe that long before the year 2000 A.D. [*sic*], and very probably before 1950, a successful aeroplane will have soared and come home safe and sound.

H. G. Wells, 1901

WAR

War

The Nature of War

Five great enemies to peace inhabit with us—avarice, ambition, envy, anger, and pride. If those enemies were to be banished, we should infallibly enjoy perpetual peace.

Petrarch

It is apparently not possible for another real war among the nations of Europe to take place.

David Starr Jordan, 1914

We live in a world where emergencies are always possible, and our survival may depend on our capacity to meet emergencies. Having said that, it is necessary also to say that emergency measures—however good for the emergency—do not make good permanent policies. Emergency measures are costly, they are superficial, and they imply that the enemy has the initiative.

John Foster Dulles

Soldiers usually are close students of tactics, but rarely are they students of strategy and practically never of war.

Bernard Brodie

War is part of the intercourse of the human race.

War is the province of danger, and therefore courage above all things is the first quality of the warrior.

War is the province of physical exertion and suffering.

War is the province of uncertainty.

War is the province of friction.

War demands resolution, firmness, and staunchness.

> Ernest Hemingway
> *Men at War* (chapter titles), quoting Carl von Clausewitz

Air power is particularly vulnerable to the perils of strategy made by rule of thumb. Its potential cannot be judged nearly as well by historical precedent as both critics and advocates would like: its utility depends much more on the particulars of the case than they might think.

> Eliot A. Cohen, 1995

It just worries the hell out of me. It's damned easy to get in war, but it's going to be awfully hard to ever extricate yourself if you do get in.

> Pres. Lyndon B. Johnson, 27 May 1964, telephone conversation with National Security Advisor McGeorge Bundy

The purpose of all war is peace.

> Augustine

In order for a war to be just, three things are necessary. Firstly, the authority of the sovereign. . . . Secondly, a just cause. . . . Thirdly, . . . a rightful intention.

Thomas Aquinas

The supreme excellence is not to win a hundred victories. The supreme excellence is to subdue the armies of your enemies without having to fight them.

Sun Tzu

In war, Resolution; in defeat, Defiance; in victory, Magnanimity.

Winston Churchill

One thing stands out clearly against the background of my experience: the winning of peace is much more difficult than the winning of even a global war. . . . . The principles of yesterday no longer apply. Air travel, air-power, air transportation of troops and supplies have changed the whole picture. We must think in terms of tomorrow. . . . Let us give the people of the United States the best, the most efficient, the most modernly equipped armed forces possible, using as determining factors, our foreign policy and the capabilities and limitations of our enemies.

Hap Arnold

Nobody dislikes war more than warriors, but we value the causes of peace so highly that we will not duck a war in an effort to get a lasting peace.

Gen Daniel "Chappie" James Jr.

That slaughter is a horrifying spectacle must make us take war more seriously, but that doesn't excuse blunting our swords in the name of humanity. Sooner or later someone with a sharp sword will come along and cut off our arms.

Carl von Clausewitz

Clausewitz on Policy and War

Now the first, the grandest, and most decisive act of judgment which the Statesman and General exercises is rightly to understand in this respect the war in which he engages, not to take it for something, or wish to make of it something, which by the nature of its relations it is impossible for it to be.

The ultimate object of our wars, the political one, is not always quite a simple one.

The great point is to keep the overruling relations of both parties in view. Out of them a certain center of gravity, a center of power and movement, will form itself, on which all depends.

Truth alone is but a weak motive of action with men, and hence there is always a great difference between knowing and action, between science and art.

Where no powerful motives press and drive, cabinets will not risk much in the game. The more war becomes in this manner devitalized so much the more its theory becomes desti-

tute of the necessary firm pivots and but-
tresses for reasoning.

Where judgment begins, there art begins.

Clausewitz

War as Art and Science

The terrain of war is generally mapped using one of two "projections": those of art and science. As with other maps, detailed study of both projections leads to more complete understanding of the terrain.

War

The science of war (knowledge).
The art of war (application of knowledge).

> Wallace P. Franz and Harry G. Summers
> *Art of War Colloquium,* textbook
> Army War College

It is absolutely true in war, were other things equal, that numbers—whether men, shells, bombs, etc.—would be supreme. Yet it is also absolutely true that other things are never equal and can never be equal. There is always a difference, and it is the differences which by begging to differ so frequently throw all calculations to the winds.

> J. F. C. Fuller

War belongs not to the province of Arts and Sciences, but to the province of social life. It is a conflict of great interests, which is settled by bloodshed, and only in that is it different from others. It would be better, instead of comparing it with any Art, to liken it to business competition, which is also a conflict of human interests and activities; and it is still more like State policy, which, again, can be looked upon as a kind of business competition on a great scale.

Clausewitz

The art of war teaches us to rely not on the likelihood of the enemy not coming, but on our own readiness to receive him.

Sun Tzu

War involves in its progress such a train of unforeseen and unsupposed circumstances that no human wisdom can calculate the end. It has but one thing certain, and that is to increase taxes.

Thomas Paine

War and truth have a fundamental incompatibility. The devotion to secrecy in the interests of the military machine largely explains why, throughout history, its operations commonly appear in retrospect the most uncertain and least efficient of human activities.

B. H. Liddell Hart

If I always appear prepared, it is because before entering on an undertaking, I have meditated for long and have foreseen what may occur. It is not genius which reveals to me suddenly and secretly what I should do in circumstances unexpected by others; it is thought and preparation.

Napoléon

Time and Space

Time is necessary to both belligerents, . . .
the only question is: which of the two, judg-
ing by his position, has most reason to expect *special advantages* from time?

Clausewitz

When you engage in actual fighting, if victory
is long in coming, the men's weapons will
grow dull and their ardour dampened. Again,
if the campaign is protracted the resources of
the State will not be equal to the strain. Thus,
though we have heard of stupid haste in war,
cleverness has never been associated with
long delays. There is no instance of a country
having benefitted from prolonged warfare.

Sun Tzu

Time is the condition to be won to defeat the
enemy. Time ranks first among the three factors necessary for victory, coming before terrain and support of the people. Only with
time can we defeat the enemy.

Ho Chi Minh

Space in which to maneuver in the air, unlike fighting on land or sea, is practically
unlimited.

Group Captain J. E. "Johnnie" Johnson

You can't expect the Rapid Reaction Force to be ready immediately.

Military spokesman on preparations for
Implementation Force

You win battles by knowing the enemy's timing, and using a timing which the enemy does not expect.

Miyamoto Musashi

At the outset of a war, time is the supreme factor. Do not let us forget that the aggressor is also concerned with the time factor; he is ready, otherwise he would not have provoked armed conflict; he inevitably hopes and plans for a quick decision, since no one would wish for a long war if it could be avoided; moreover he wants a decision before his opponent has had time to "turn his capacity into the new activities which war calls for."

Lord Tedder

Go sir, gallop, and don't forget that the world was made in six days. You can ask me for anything you like, except time.

Napoléon

A good plan executed *now* is better than a perfect plan next week.

GEN George S. Patton

Never interrupt your enemy when he is making a mistake.

Napoléon

Rapidity is the essence of war; take advantage of the enemy's unreadiness, make your way by unexpected routes, and attack unguarded spots.

Sun Tzu

The last war is not modern, it is out of date. At the same time there are factors that do not change, or only change very slowly. Geography does not change—though its effect on military operations may be modified by technical changes. Human nature does not change, and national characteristics and temperaments change but slowly. Economic factors, generally speaking, change slowly.

Lord Tedder

If there is one attitude more dangerous than to assume that a future war will be just like the last one, it is to imagine that it will be so utterly different that we can afford to ignore all the lessons of the last one.

J. C. Slessor, 1936

But there is one element in relation to the flying machine that we are not producing, that we cannot produce in an emergency, and that is the men. We can produce machines but not the aviators. That takes time.

Alexander Graham Bell

Strategy is the art of making use of time and space. Space we can recover; lost time, never.

Napoléon

He who can move twice as fast as his opponent doubles his operative time and thereby halves that of his opponent.

J. F. C. Fuller

Effects

But there is another way. It is possible to increase the likelihood of success without defeating the enemy's forces. I refer to operations that have direct political repercussions, that are designed in the first place to disrupt the opposing alliance, or to paralyze it, that gain us new allies, favorably affect the political scene, etc. If such operations are possible it is obvious that they can greatly improve our prospects and that they can form a much shorter route to the goal than the destruction of the opposing armies.

Clausewitz
On War, book 1, chapter 2

Objectives are essential to achieve unity of effort. In the abstract sense, the objective is the effect desired.

Joint Publication 0-2, *Unified Action Armed Forces*, 1995

The significance of the capacity to affect a large number of objectives simultaneously in the Gulf War was not simply that a lot of targets could be attacked, but that vital enemy systems could be brought under effective control.

Brig Gen David A. Deptula, 2001

The cause is hidden but the effect is known.

Ovid
Metamorphoses IV, ca. AD 5

The most important events are often determined by very trivial causes.

> Cicero
> *Orationes Philippicae* V, 60 BC

In past air campaigns, the random effects of
ballistic weapons often created ambiguity and
uncertainty as to intent. We can now expect
enemies to rapidly assess the pattern of targets attacked by PGMs in an effort to predict
future attacks. This suggests that we need to
contemplate the second-order effects of force
application—human responses and target
system responses—rather than just the immediate effects we intend to achieve. Understanding what up to now have been "unin-
tended effects" is just a first step; airmen
need to plan and perhaps even devise strategy
around them. All the processes of adjusting
to air attack (e.g., dispersing, digging in, moving, reorganizing) cost the enemy something
and may deserve consideration as campaign
objectives in themselves.

> Lt Gen Charles G. Boyd, 1991

The effects of an attack against the industrial
facilities on the social life of a nation cannot be
overestimated. Modern warfare places an enormous load upon the economic system of a nation which increases its sensitivity to attack.

> "Air Force Objectives"
> Air Corps Tactical School lecture, 1935

Only by a careful analysis—by painstaking investigation—will it be possible to select the line of action that will make it possible to efficiently employ the air force during war. It is a study for the statistician, the technical expert, not the soldier.

"National Economic Structures"
Air Corps Tactical School lecture, 1936

Well before it makes any sense to talk about mechanics, it is imperative to decide what effect you want to produce on the enemy. Making this decision is the toughest intellectual challenge; once the desired effect is decided, figuring out how to attain it is much easier if for no other reason than we practice the necessary tactical events every day, whereas we rarely (far too rarely) think about strategic and operational problems. Let us propose a very simple rule for how to go about producing the effect: do it very fast.

Col John A. Warden III, 1996

The "Revolution in Military Affairs" is now the mantra of those who seek remote, clinical, and surgical solutions to what has traditionally been a close-in, chaotic, and bloody brawl. This has weakened the concept of the warrior, as the androgynous technician has gained ascendancy in some quarters.

LtGen Bernard E. "Mick" Trainor, USMC, retired, 2000

I believe that effects-based operations will be the doctrinal concept—the future joint war-fighting concept—that our nation will employ. But it ain't ready yet.

GEN William F. Kernan, 2002

Strategy

Strategy is the employment of battle to gain the end in war; it must therefore give an aim to the whole military action, which must be in accordance with the object of the war; in other words, strategy forms the plan of the war.

Clausewitz

Tactics are concerned with doing the job "right," higher levels of strategy are concerned with doing the "right" job.

Dennis M. Drew and Donald M. Snow

Throughout his life Alexander consistently subordinated strategy to policy, which is the essence of grand strategy.

J. F. C. Fuller

The strategist is he who always keeps the objective of the war in sight and the objective of the war is never military and is always political.

Alfred Thayer Mahan

The twin problems of modern warfare: How to persuade the adversary to come to terms without inflicting on him such severe damage as to prejudice all chances of subsequent stability and peace? Under what circumstances can armed force be used, in the only way in which it can be legitimate to use it, to ensure a lasting and stable peace?

Sir Michael Howard

The soundest strategy is to postpone operations until the moral disintegration of the enemy renders the delivery of the mortal blow both possible and easy.

Vladimir I. Lenin

Fight the enemy with the weapons he lacks.

Aleksandr V. Suvorov

True economy of force is using the indirect approach to effect a psychological defeat without engaging in actual combat.

B. H. Liddell Hart

In Japan there was nothing that could be called grand or military strategy until a short time before the outbreak of World War II. There was little correlation between her national defense theory and the strategic plans of the army and the navy. In [my opinion this] eventually resulted in the calamity of Japan entering into her disastrous war.

Japanese historian Toshiyuki Yokoi

Generally in war the best policy is to take a state intact; to ruin it is inferior to this. To capture the enemy's army is better than to destroy it. To subdue the enemy without fighting is the acme of skill. Thus, what is of extreme importance in war is to attack the enemy's strategy; next best is to disrupt his alliances; [and] next best is to attack his forces. The worst policy is to attack his cities; do so only when there is no alternative.

Sun Tzu

Where the strategist is empowered to seek a military decision, his responsibility is to seek it under the most advantageous circumstances in order to produce the most profitable result. *Hence his true aim is not so much to seek battle as to seek a strategic situation so advantageous that if it does not of itself produce the decision, its continuation by battle is sure to achieve this.*

B. H. Liddell Hart

1. He will win who knows when to fight and when not to fight.

2. He will win who knows how to handle both superior and inferior forces.

3. He will win whose army is animated by the same spirit throughout all the ranks.

4. He will win who, prepared himself, waits to take the enemy unprepared.

5. He will win who has military capacity and is not interfered with by the sovereign.

Victory lies in the knowledge of these five points.

Sun Tzu

It is the mark of good action that it appears inevitable in retrospect.

Robert Louis Stevenson

There are some roads not to follow; some troops not to strike; some cities not to assault; and some ground which should not be contested.

Sun Tzu

We must perceive the necessity of every war being looked upon as a whole from the very outset, and that at the very first step forward the commander should have the end in view to which every line must converge.

Clausewitz

In war the victorious strategist seeks battle after the victory has been won, whereas he who is destined to defeat first fights and afterwards looks to victory.

Sun Tzu

Deterrence

To be prepared for war is one of the most effectual means of preserving peace.

George Washington

The expenses required to prevent a war are much lighter than those that will, if not prevented, be absolutely necessary to maintain it.

Benjamin Franklin

It is customary in democratic countries to deplore expenditure on armament as conflicting with the requirements of the social services. There is a tendency to forget that the most important social service that a government can do for its people is to keep them alive and free.

J. C. Slessor

The great lesson to be learned in the battered towns of England and the ruined cities of Germany is that the best way to win a war is to prevent it from occurring. That must be the ultimate end to which our best efforts are devoted. It has been suggested—and wisely so—that this objective is well served by insuring the strength and security of the United States. The United States was founded and has since lived upon principles of tolerance, freedom, and goodwill at home and abroad. Strength based on these principles is no threat to world peace. Prevention of war will not come from neglect of strength or lack of foresight or alertness on our part. Those who contemplate evil and aggression find encouragement in such neglect. Hitler relied heavily upon it.

> US Strategic Bombing Survey
> Summary Report (Europe)

If we are living in a world where either side can make a surprise attack upon the other which destroys the latter's capability to make a meaningful retaliation, then it makes sense to be trigger-happy with one's strategic air power. But if, on the other hand, the situation is such that neither side can hope to eliminate the retaliatory power of the other, that restraint which was suicidal in one situation now becomes prudence, and it is trigger-happiness that becomes suicidal.

> Bernard Brodie

It is a doctrine of war not to assume the enemy will not come, but rather to rely on one's readiness to meet him; not to presume that he will not attack, but rather to make one's self invincible.

> Sun Tzu

America must maintain a state of readiness for defense and counterattack. This is not just for the sake of being prepared. Of equal or greater importance is the fact that the *visi-*

bility of our preparedness will deter attacks against us.

Gen Curtis E. LeMay

Forces that cannot win will not deter.

Gen Nathan F. Twining

Deterrence is not just aircraft on alert and missiles in the silos. It is not defined by the size of the defense budget. It is a product of both capability and credibility.

Gen Jerome F. O'Malley

A nation, regardless of its protestations, if it feels that its national existence is threatened and that it is losing a war, will turn to any weapon that it can use.

GEN Walter Bedell Smith

There will always be time enough to die; like a drowning man who will clutch instinctively at a straw, it is the natural law of the moral world that a nation that finds itself on the brink of an abyss will try to save itself by any means.

Clausewitz

When you surround an army, leave an outlet free. Do not press a desperate foe too hard.

Sun Tzu

Irregular Warfare

By exacting a great price on the Taliban for any massing of forces to defend or counter-attack, the asymmetrical advantage of the US ground-based targeting and air attack made the ground forces of the Northern Alliance unstoppable.

GEN Montgomery C. Meigs, USA, retired, 2003

We are no more prepared for the suicidal "human bomb" terrorist in the Middle East than we were for the saffron-robed monk in Saigon who put the torch to himself. . . . We persist in refusing to acknowledge what we don't know or understand about them—or heaven forbid—to concede that many of them are not likely to respond to either our threats or our blandishments.

Meg Greenfield, 1983

In point of fact you do not control a country from the air, any more than from the business end of a gun. It is the civil administrator, the District Commissioner or Political Officer, and the policeman who control the country.

J. C. Slessor, 1957

It is fighting at a great disadvantage to fight those who have nothing to lose.

> Francesco Guicciardini
> *Storia d'Italia*, 1564

The conventional army loses if it does not win. The guerrilla wins if he does not lose.

> Henry Kissinger

Perhaps the only subject regarding the American intervention [in Nicaragua] upon which all authorities are able to agree is the efficacy with which the Marines employed the air power at their disposal.

> Lejeune Cummins
> *Quijote on a Burro*, 1958

Our evidence goes to show that it is not the way force is applied but its effectiveness that is feared and to that extent resented. Once force is actually applied, the tribesm[a]n probably dislike[s] land and air operations equally, except that in the latter his prized inaccessibility is taken from him and his opportunities for hitting back are far more limited.

> Rufus Isaacs, Lord Reading, 1925

Lessons from RAF Operations in Iraq, 1914–32

- Perhaps the most serious long term consequence of the ready availability of air control was that it developed into a substitute for administration.

- The speed and simplicity of air attack was preferred to the more time consuming and painstaking investigation of grievances and disputes.

- With such powers at its disposal the Iraq Government was not encouraged to develop less violent methods of extending its control over the country.

Peter Sluglett, 1976

Those governments that were able to create effective intelligence organizations and use them efficiently were normally successful in their counterinsurgency efforts. This was particularly true of the British campaign in Malaya from 1948 to 1960 and the Philippine operations against the Huks from 1946 to 1954. In both instances, accurate and timely intelligence was a crucial factor in defeating the insurgents. On the other hand, inadequate intelligence was a significant weakness in the French campaign against the Viet Minh in Indochina.

Dr. Charles A. Russell and
Maj Robert E. Hildner, 1973

So far from the use of the aeroplane having tended to replace the intimate knowledge of the local Political Officer regarding his tribes, it has done an enormous amount towards increasing that knowledge and towards removing the risk of inflicting indiscriminate punishment on the innocent and guilty alike.

Sir Steuart Pears
Resident in Waziristan, 1924

The tenets of AirLand Battle apply equally to the military operations characteristic of low intensity war.

Army Field Manual 100-5, *Operations*, 1986

One of the most significant after effects of the September 11, 2001 attacks on the World Trade Center in New York has been the realization that anti-terrorism operations will now be occupying the center stage of military operations for at least the next few years, if not decades.

Air Commodore Tariq Mahmud Ashraf
Pakistan air force

Friction, War's Resistant Medium

Everything is very simple in war, but the simplest thing is difficult. These difficulties accumulate and produce a friction which no man can imagine exactly who has not seen war.

Clausewitz

If one has never personally experienced war, one cannot understand in what the difficulties constantly mentioned really consist, nor why a commander should need any brilliance and exceptional ability.

Clausewitz

Only the study of military history is capable of giving those who have no experience of their own a clear picture of what I have just called the friction of the whole machine.

Clausewitz

War is composed of nothing but accidents, and though holding to general principles, a general should never lose sight of everything to enable him to profit from these accidents; that is the mark of genius.

Napoléon

War is the realm of uncertainty; three quarters of the factors on which action in war is based are wrapped in a fog of greater or lesser uncertainty. A sensitive and discriminating judgment is called for: a skilled intelligence to scent out the truth.

Clausewitz

Clausewitz framed the notion of friction in On War, *book 1, chapter 7.*

Oils for the
Friction of War

Now is there, then, no kind of oil which is capable of diminishing this friction? Only one, and that one is not always available at the will of the Commander or his Army. It is the habituation of an Army to War.

Clausewitz

Clausewitz corrected the notion that habituation was the sole remedy for the friction of war by prescribing leadership as a second remedy. Other remedies include: understanding war's uncertainty; professional training; exercises that include friction; war games and thought exercises; maintaining alternatives; maintaining reserves; plans that provide room for frictional results; mental agility; organizational agility; clarity of purpose; judicious use of the initiative; and the compound lubricants of mental clarity, originality, discipline, and doctrine.

The more one can increase the fog and friction encountered by the enemy, the more likely it is that the enemy will be defeated. Flexible plans with alternative objectives, counterintelligence, disinformation deception, concealment, and campaigns to disrupt [the] enemy . . . not only lead to serious errors by the enemy on the battlefield but can also cause confusion and uncertainty that

lower morale, sap aggressiveness, cause ten-
tativeness, and undermine initiative.

Dennis Drew and Donald Snow

*The friction of war stems from the magni-
fied results of fundamental uncertainties.*

You will usually find that the enemy has
three courses open to him, and of these he
will adopt the fourth.

Moltke, the Elder

A battle sometimes decides everything; and
sometimes the most trifling thing decides the
fate of a battle.

Napoléon

In wars throughout history, events have generally proved the pre-hostilities calculations
of both sides, victor as well as loser, to have
been seriously wrong.

Bernard Brodie

All action in war is directed on probable, not
certain, results. Whatever is wanting in cer-
tainty must always be left to fate, or chance,
call it which you will. We may demand that
what is so left should be as little as possible,
but only in relation to the particular case—
that is, as little as possible in this one case,
but not that the case in which the least is left
to chance is always to be preferred. That

would be an enormous error. There are cases in which the greatest daring is the greatest wisdom.

Clausewitz

The Art of Studying Circumstances

To refrain from intercepting an enemy whose banners are in perfect order, to refrain from attacking an army drawn up in calm and confident array—this is the art of studying circumstances.

Sun Tzu

The most important thing is to have a flexible approach. . . . The truth is no one knows exactly what air fighting will be like in the future. We can't say anything will stay as it is, but we also can't be sure the future will conform to particular theories, which so often, between the wars, have proved wrong.

Brig Gen Robin Olds

In his many battles his tactical genius is apparent in the lightning-like speed with which he adapted his actions to novel circumstances.

J. F. C. Fuller on Alexander the Great

The problem for the military planner is that intentions can change far more rapidly than can capability. A military capability can take a decade to develop while an election, or a coup-d'etat, can change political intentions overnight. Of all the factors which allow an airman to rapidly redirect his efforts in such circumstances the greatest is range, or more, descriptively, reach.

Air Vice-Marshal J. R. "Johnnie" Walker, RAF

The more I see of war, the more I realize how it all depends on administration and transportation.

Field Marshal Earl A. P. Wavell

The carrying out of a plan, from its very beginning to the conclusion of an operation, is another process of knowing the situation; i.e., the process of putting it into practice. In this process, there is need to examine anew whether the plan corresponds with the actualities. If the plan does not correspond or does not fully correspond with them, then we must, according to fresh knowledge, form new judgments and make new decisions to modify the original plan in order to meet the new situation.

Mao Tse-tung

It is above all necessary that a general should adopt a role proportionate to his capacity, a plan that he feels himself able to follow out methodically amidst dangers, surprise, friction, accidents of all sorts.

Jean Colin

The truths of war are absolute, but the principles governing their application have to be deduced on each occasion from the circumstances, which are always different.

Winston Churchill

One falls into a feeling of security by mental laziness and through lack of calculation concerning the intentions of the enemy. To proceed properly it is necessary to put oneself in his place and say: What would I do if I were the enemy? What project would I form? Make as many as possible of these projects, examine them all, and above all reflect on the means to avert them. But do not let these calculations make you timid. Circumspection is good only up to a certain point.

Frederick the Great

OUTCOMES
AND
ARGUMENTS

Outcomes
and
Arguments

Operation Desert Storm

You have restored my confidence in the United States Air Force. CENTAF [Central Command Air Forces] can't do [the] planning. Do it the way you want. It is up to the Air Force. . . . I love it. You are the first guys who are leaning forward. This is exactly what I want.

> GEN Norman Schwarzkopf to Col John Warden regarding initial Instant Thunder air campaign plan for Iraq, 10 August 1990

In the end, of course, the Gulf War did in fact include a strategic air campaign, and the very least that one could say about it was that by so thoroughly destroying the Iraqis' capability to wage warfare, it permitted a relatively bloodless war-concluding ground operation by coalition army forces. The most one could say about the air campaign was that it—in and of itself—won the war.

> Gen Charles G. Boyd

It is undeniable that for six weeks—during the period now known as the air campaign— coalition aircraft dropped tons of bombs and missiles on Iraqi targets. It is also undeniable that Iraq's ground forces were totally ineffective against the coalition's ground forces. But those facts do not prove that the bombing caused Iraqi ineffectiveness.

> Daryl Press, Dartmouth College

I don't always find that Desert Storm receives the historical, honest perspective that it should. In fact, it tends to be a gold mine that people go to to extract particular points they want to make and then justify, based on that war. In fact, I go to briefing after briefing from my own space people who tell me how they won the Gulf War. . . . I sit there and smile and say, "Thank you very much. I appreciate that."

Gen Charles A. Horner, 1993

Desert Storm Air Campaign objectives

- Gain and maintain air supremacy to permit unhindered air and ground operations.

- Isolate and incapacitate the Iraqi regime.

- Destroy Iraq's known NBC [nuclear, biological, chemical] warfare capability.

- Eliminate Iraq's offensive military capability by destroying key military production, infrastructure, and power capabilities.

- Render the Iraqi army and its mechanized equipment in Kuwait ineffective, causing its collapse.

Department of Defense, *Conduct of the Persian Gulf War: Final Report to Congress*, 1992

The recent air campaign against Iraqi forces gained not a single one of the US or UN [United Nations] objectives in the Persian Gulf War. Four days of land combat—aided immeasurably by the air campaign—achieved every goal and victory.

GEN Frederick J. Kroesen, USA, retired, 1994

The desert—a tactician's paradise, a quarter-master's nightmare.

Attributed to a German general

Out of 2,400 main battle tanks, 1,865 were destroyed by Coalition airpower. This does not include Iraqi tanks destroyed by US Army Aviation.

Col Viktor Patzalyuk
Former Soviet military attaché to Baghdad

The Multinational Forces [MNF] won the war back before the beginning of the ground offensive as a result of an almost 40-day offensive air operation. . . . The concentration of an MNF ground army of a half million indicates the US command did not believe it would be able to win the war without its use.

Russian colonel (Reserve) Yu. G. Sizov and Col A. L. Skokov, 1993

The Gulf War brought to the fore the technology, tactics, techniques, and operational methods on which the Air Force had been working since the Vietnam War. Precision guided munitions, precision navigation systems like the global positioning system (GPS), and day-night all-weather operations allowed the Air Force to fly, fight, and win in the face of the worst weather in the Middle East in more than a decade. That technology helped to win the fastest, lowest casualty, most devastatingly destructive one-sided war in recorded history. Air Force capabilities had come of age.

James A. Mowbray, 1995

The air war against Iraq turned out to be an enormous success. One of the reasons for this triumph was the integration of the various air forces into a solid fighting force.

Miron Rezun, 1992

Allied air supremacy in Desert Storm created conditions that could with equal facility have been exploited by a frontal assault, a flanking attack of almost any magnitude, an airborne insertion almost anywhere, or an amphibious assault—or some combination of the four. Aerospace supremacy thus preserved ambiguity of intent, and with it, strategic maneuverability and surprise for all force types.

Air Force Manual (AFM) 1-1, *Basic Aerospace Doctrine of the United States Air Force*, vol. 2, 1992

The sheer abundance of assets such as aircraft, airfields, and tankers allowed the air campaign generally to accommodate all service points of view on the priorities of the air war.

Congressmen Les Aspin and William L. Dickinson, 1992

This way I didn't have to play around with the [joint air planning] process while I was waiting to hit a target. I kind of gamed the [air tasking order] process. The Navy's trouble was that they tried to do it honestly and write just what they were going to fly.

MajGen Royal N. Moore Jr., USMC, 1991

The Coalition was fortunate to have an overwhelming number of air forces in the Gulf War. When elements of one force component chose to bypass the joint air planning process, the JFACC [joint force air component commander], in the interest of avoiding doctrinal strife, could afford to rely upon forces

Outcomes and Arguments

103

directly under his command to accomplish theater objectives.

Brig Gen David A. Deptula, 2001

If an Iraqi pilot had managed to penetrate the airspace above the border area during the great shift west, he would have been stunned by the panorama below. It was mile after mile of tank transporters, gasoline tankers, troop and ammunition carriers. . . . I shudder to think what a couple of Iraqi planes could have done to that column on a strafing and bombing run.

COL David Hackworth, 1991

Iraq's operational center of gravity, the Republican Guard, and to a lesser extent, the heavy divisions of the regular army, remained a viable fighting force in spite of significant physical damage caused by air attack because their will to fight was not broken. Only by vanquishing an enemy and displacing him on the ground can a military force break the enemy's will and ensure ultimate victory.

Robert H. Scales, Terry L. Johnson, and
Thomas P. Odom, 1993

There had never been a war like that before and the wonder is that, in what was in effect a military laboratory, the workers and their apparatus so often achieved the correct results. It is odd that Americans now seem as

eager to decry their victory in the Gulf as they
were their defeat in Vietnam.

John Keegan

For the Army, the JFACC system was a beast
to be tamed. . . . An Army corps commander
was not concerned with the entire theater.
He looked at the battlefield like a giant bowl-
ing alley. To move down the lane, the corps
needed to sweep the obstacles from its path,
starting with those directly in front of it and
then those a day or two away. For the corps
commanders, air power was a form of flying
artillery and should be on call immediately to
support their attack.

Michael Gordon and
LtGen Mick Trainor, USMC, retired, 1995

The parallel attack against Iraq was against
what may well have been the country best
prepared in all the world for attack. The Iraqi
army was the largest fielded since the Chinese in the Korean War.

Col John A. Warden III, 1996

It is a given that air power theory is enjoying
a renaissance that is completely unrealistic
in light of the reality of the Gulf War or of
capabilities achievable in any reasonable
timeframe.

GEN Gordon Sullivan
Chief of Staff, US Army, 1994

Evidence from the Gulf War suggests that even if there had been no significant air campaign, the ground war would not have been substantially different.

Daryl Press, Dartmouth College

We may require a sterner test against a more capable adversary to come to a conclusive judgment. But if air power again exerts similar dominance over opposing ground forces, the conclusion will be inescapable that some threshold in the relationship between air and ground forces was first crossed in Desert Storm.

Thomas A. Keaney and Eliot Cohen, 1995

To a great extent, information combat has been enlightened by the Gulf War, in which multinational troops captured all the high-frequency and ultrahigh frequency radio signals of the Iraqi army and stored the numerous amounts of information gathered by the 34 reconnaissance satellites, 260 electronic reconnaissance planes, and 40 prewarning aircraft. Then, the multinational troops used various information systems and high-tech weapons to destroy the Iraqi communication system and take control of the war. The Iraqi command system, radar, and command systems of missiles, aircraft, and artillery were at a standstill. This demonstrates that information is the key to victory. The side that controls information can give full play to the materials and energy possessed, and thereby increase combat power.

Maj Gen Zheng Shenxia and
Senior Col Zhang Changzi, PLAAF, 1996

Operation Deliberate Force (Bosnia)

U.S. air strikes delivered 1,026 bombs against 56 military targets in western Bosnia and near Sarajevo—less than half the munitions used per day against Saddam's army in the Persian Gulf War, but enough to debilitate the far smaller and less heavily armed Bosnian Serb Army.

Robert A. Pape, 2004

One of the great things that people should have learned from this is that there are times when air power—not backed up by ground troops—can make a difference.

Amb. Richard Holbrooke, 1996

So much damage from such a little thing.

Slobodan Milosevic, overheard looking at an Air Force cruise missile at the Air Force Museum, 1995

In the past we thought about precision in terms of meters CEP, Circular Error Probable. Now we should think in terms of the precise application of military effect to policy objectives. That's what that Bosnia campaign sort of unveiled.

Maj Gen Chuck Link, 1996

Air power not only was the lead arm of American involvement in the region but also was almost certainly the only politically viable offensive arm available for use by the United States and any of its partners.

Col Robert C. Owen, 2000

We don't need to occupy an enemy's country to defeat his strategy. We can reduce his combat capabilities and in many instances defeat his armed forces from the air.

Gen Ronald R. Fogleman

In 1994 and 1995 President Clinton . . . had many options to deal with these crises—capabilities beyond silver bullets that would not work then and will not work tomorrow. It was forces on the ground with balanced full spectrum dominance that successfully secured U.S. interests.

GEN Dennis J. Reimer, 1996

Inserting ground forces in a region today may create more problems than it resolves.

Richard Hallion
"Airpower and the Changing Nature of Warfare"

If those calls for air strikes against the Serbs had been heeded in 1992, Holbrooke suggests, some two million refugees would probably today be in their homes and at least 100,000 lives might have been saved. An

early and large intervention by NATO war-
planes, something that did not occur until the
fall of 1995, might even have accomplished
what will probably never be accomplished
now, the rebuilding of a viable, multiethnic
Bosnian state.

Chris Hedges
New York Times, 1998

While normal procedure called for attacking
aircraft to minimize their exposure to enemy
defensive systems by dropping all of their
weapons in single passes, General Ryan required many aircraft over Bosnia to make
multiple passes, dropping only one weapon
at a time, and only after the dust from previous weapons had cleared. These tactics exposed crews to the potential of ground de-
fenders improving their aim with practice,
but they also assured that all bombs were
released as accurately as possible and in no
greater number than was required to destroy
a target. In other instances, targets were hit
late at night to minimize the likelihood that
civilians and even military personnel would
be in or on them.

Col Robert C. Owen, 2001

Operation Allied Force
(Kosovo)

There are certain dates in the history of war-fare that mark real turning points. Now there is a new turning point to fix on the calendar: June 3, 1999, when the capitulation of President Milosevic proved that a war can be won by air power alone . . . the air forces have won a triumph, are entitled to every plaudit they will receive and can look forward to enjoying a transformed status in the strategic community, one they have earned by their single-handed efforts. All this can be said without reservation, and should be conceded by the doubters, of whom I was one, with generosity. . . . This was a victory through air power.

John Keegan, 1999

They knew everything about us. There wasn't anything they didn't know. If we lit a cigarette they could see it. God knows what they were dropping on us, all sorts of bombs. We didn't expect that intensity.

"Milos," a Yugoslavian soldier
Quoted by Rory Carroll, 1999

While NATO leaders and planners may have believed that they were communicating some sort of message to Milosevic through bombing, on the ground the message could hardly be extracted from the background noise.

William M. Arkin, 2000

Attacking fielded enemy forces without the shaping presence of a NATO ground threat had produced "major challenges," including creating a faster flexible targeting cycle; putting a laser designator on Predator; creating new target development processes within the [combined air operations center]; creating real-time communications links between finders, assessors, and shooters; and developing more real-time retargeting procedures.

Gen John Jumper

Airpower alone has never been decisive. In Vietnam, for example, the Air Force dropped some 6 million tons of bombs, almost triple the tonnage dropped in World War II, without breaking the North Vietnamese will to resist.

COL Harry Summers, USA, retired, 1999

The battle damage assessment of strikes against individual ground weapons remains as much an uncertain art form as during the Gulf War in spite of advances in [unmanned aerial vehicles], reconnaissance and intelligence systems, and analysis. NATO and the US lack the capability to "close the loop" in terms of reliable, real-time battle damage assessment

that can be used for effective tactical decision making.

Anthony H. Cordesman, 1999

I found myself reiterating our priorities again
and again. "You must impact the Serb Forces
on the ground. Do you understand that attacking the Serb forces on the ground is my
top priority? We're going to win or lose this
campaign based on how well we go after the
ground targets."

GEN Wesley K. Clark, USA, retired, 2001

The tank, which was an irrelevant item in the
context of ethnic cleansing, became the sym-
bol of Serbian ground forces. How many
tanks did you kill today: All of a sudden, this
became the measure of merit although it had
nothing to do with reality.

Gen Joe Ralston

[Precision-guided munitions] can offset the
need for mass attacks to achieve a high probability of success—a reality evidenced with the
dramatic increase of their use in the air war
over Serbia.

Brig Gen David A. Deptula, 2001

For the first time in some 5,000 years of military history—5,000 years of history of man
taking organized forces into combat—we saw
an independent air operation produce a po-

litical result. What that means for the future we will still have to divine. . . . This kind of utility can do nothing but place greater demands on air and space forces for the future.

Gen Mike Dugan, USAF, retired, 1999

Both of these attributes of air power—relatively low force vulnerability and high precision—can also fortify coalition unity, which is itself susceptible to disruptions as friendly casualties and collateral damage mount.

Daniel L. Byman and Matthew C. Waxman, 2000

Planning and preparations for ground intervention were well under way by the end of the campaign, and I am convinced that this, in particular, pushed Milosevic to concede.

GEN Wesley K. Clark, USA, retired, 2001

To move Task Force Hawk to its location at an airfield in Rinas, Albania, required 550 C-17 sorties. . . . Task Force Hawk was built around 24 AH-64 attack helicopters. . . . To command the unit, a corps headquarters deployed from Germany.

Michael G. Vickers, 2001

The reason Slobodan Milosevic finally caved in—a primary reason—was the presence of US Army ground forces in Albania.

LTG John W. Hendrix, 1999

Already some of the critics of the war are indulging in ungracious revisionism, suggest-
ing that we have not witnessed a strategic
revolution and that Milosevic was humbled
by the threat to deploy ground troops or by
the processes of traditional diplomacy. . . .
All to be said to that is that diplomacy had
not worked before March 24, when the bombing started, while the deployment of a large
ground force, though clearly a growing threat,
would still have taken weeks to accomplish
at the moment Milosevic caved in. The revi-
sionists are wrong. This was a victory through
air power.

John Keegan, 1999

I would have argued for a campaign that, if it
couldn't include ground troops, then don't
take away also the threat of ground troops.

GEN Colin Powell, USA, retired, 1999

Only institutional pride would maintain that
there is only one formula for subduing an
enemy.

William M. Arkin, 2000

Operation Enduring Freedom (2001–)

Four simple words describe our mission: global strike, precision engagement. It's exactly on the other side of the globe from Missouri. It's a long way.

Brig Gen Anthony F. Przybyslawski, 2001

Outcomes and Arguments

Nobody's calling us unilateral anymore. . . . We're so multilateral it keeps me up 24 hours a day checking on everybody.

Secretary of State Colin Powell, 2001

The best recent example of operational asymmetry involves the US campaign in Afghanistan. US forces entered the fray with technological superiority in sensors and space-based communications and the ability to deliver precision weapons from aircraft. Based on training, initiative, and fieldcraft, they possessed the ability to knit together new tactical techniques integrating an air operation and special forces with an indigenous formation, the Northern Alliance.

GEN Montgomery C. Meigs, USA, retired, 2003

It is not a quagmire at all. It's been three weeks that we've been engaged in this.

SecDef Donald Rumsfeld, 2001

This is not a rout, it is a withdrawal in reasonably good order. They don't want to hang on to any territory because if they do they will be destroyed from the air.

Charles Heyman, editor
Jane's World Armies, 2001

You must stand strong, my brothers. Don't vacate any areas. Stick to your positions and fight to the death.

Taliban leader Mullah Omar, November 2001

The success of the bombers is nevertheless a surprise, even if not a wholly unpredictable one. What had been unpredictable is the resurgence of the Northern Alliance. Their ability to achieve practical superiority, against an enemy superior in numbers who had held them at bay for five years, could not have been foreseen and defies explanation. It is not due to superior weapons—there must have been a collapse of Taliban morale.

John Keegan, 2001

What was demonstrated in Afghanistan on repeated occasion, especially early on, was not classic close air support or air interdiction but rather SOF [special operations forces]-enabled precision air attacks against enemy ground forces with no friendly ground forces in direct contact.

Ben Lambeth

This is modern war. It's not like Desert Storm. You go into it with your nose first, slowly. You get your grip. You get others to fight for you. And you use airpower as much as you can and stay as high as you can.

GEN Wesley K. Clark, USA, retired, 2001

In any scenario, the Army soldier brings closure, not precision guided munitions, not surgical strikes, and not minimalist combat events.

GEN Gordon R. Sullivan, USA, retired, 2002

Every unit that is not supported is a defeated unit.

Maurice de Saxe

Although the JFACC's staff had begun assessing the overall air effort at the beginning of the operation, CENTCOM directed that all such activities be stopped in November 2001. CENTCOM did not want independent assessments of the campaign's progress to come out of the components.

Maj Thomas J. Timmerman

Another problem in the use of U.S. air power in Afghanistan was a clear overemphasis on avoiding collateral damages. Reportedly, virtually every strike or attack was approved by CINCCENT [commander in chief, Central Command] in Tampa. Lawyers were heavily involved in approving the list of targets to be attacked, at all command echelons. The lawyers participated in determining whether a specific target was used for military purposes, evaluating the propriety of using certain type of munitions, and deciding whether a successful attack on such a target was outweighed by civilian losses. Although the commander made a final decision, this process was unnecessarily complicated, cumbersome, and time consuming.

Dr. Milan Vego, 2002

The most effective close air support asset we had was the Apache, hands down. . . . The Apaches were extraordinary—they were lethal and survivable. We had six in the fight with two left flying at the end of the first day.

MG Franklin L. Hagenbeck, 2002

Since they were unable to define what it was that they wanted from us, we just elected to . . . push on our own. . . . My answer was, I will give them more capacity than they could potentially use. I'm trying to do back-of-the-envelope planning so that even if they can't define a requirement, they will have the resources necessary to successfully execute this.

Gen John Corley, 2004

The air war in Afghanistan against a fleeting enemy operating in penny packets in extremely inhospitable terrain which made their detection very difficult demonstrated once again the tremendous flexibility and adaptability of air power to new and emerging situations. More significantly, this conflict showed that air power has a major role to play in low intensity conflicts, especially those being waged against an enemy fielding irregular forces.

Air Commodore Tariq Mahmud Ashraf
Pakistan air force

You do what you have to do, so you play the cards you're dealt. There is not one component that is dominant over the others. There are a set of components that have different tools that a combatant commander uses, and out of all of this we should have the closest of relationships because we've all walked through fire together.

Gen T. Michael Moseley, 2004

Operation Iraqi Freedom (2003–)

I do not want General McKiernan to have to stop anywhere between Kuwait and Baghdad unless it is at a local 7-11 for a chili-cheese dog and a cherry limeade.

> Lt Gen T. Michael Moseley to Combined Air Operations Center staff three days prior to Operation Iraqi Freedom

In my judgment, there should have been a minimum of two heavy divisions and an armored cavalry regiment on the ground—that's how our doctrine reads.

> GEN Barry R. McCaffrey, USA, retired, 2003

This is "Desert Lite." As they said in briefings before the war, this force is probably adequate for the job, but it doesn't leave much room for setbacks or sandstorms.

> Anthony H. Cordesman, 2003

The main thing we've learned from this is that "shock and awe" hasn't panned out. The targeting hasn't broken the back of the leadership.

> Robert A. Pape, 2003

We might be able to do the job if airpower is effective, if we don't have close contact with enemy forces, and if the Iraqi will is broken. But those are a lot of big ifs.

> GEN Wesley K. Clark, USA, retired, 2003

The Republican Guard is in full control. We have defeated them; in fact, we have crushed them. We have pushed them outside the whole area of the airport.

> Muhammad Said al-Sahhaf
> "Baghdad Bob," 6 April 2003

I believe the Americans have so far been unable to capture a single large locality because the Iraqis organized their defense using the combat experience of the Soviet Army, obtained during World War II.

> Col Gen Vladislav Achalov, Soviet army, retired, 7 April 2003

Don't believe these invaders and these liars. There are none of their troops in Baghdad.

> Muhammad Said al-Sahhaf
> "Baghdad Bob," 8 April 2003

Had it been possible to know on March 20 that in just 17 days, US forces would have captured Baghdad's international airport, destroyed most of the Republican Guard, and secured Iraq's vital oil infrastructure, all at a cost of fewer than 75 American lives, most people in this country would have been elated at the prospect of seemingly overwhelming military success.

> *Washington Post*, 6 April 2003

The divisions [Republican Guard] were essentially destroyed by airstrikes when they were still about 30 miles from their destination. . . . The Iraqi will to fight was broken outside Baghdad.

> Colonel Ghassan, Republican Guard
> Iraqi General Staff

It is difficult to overstate the importance of air operations in the context of [Operation Iraqi Freedom]. By dominating the air over Iraq, coalition air forces shaped the fight to allow for rapid dominance on the ground. . . . Integration of precision munitions with ground operations, supported by a largely space-based command and control network, enabled combat operations to occur in ways only imagined a decade ago.

> Gregory Fontenot, E. J. Degen, and David Tohn
> *On Point*, 2005

We primarily used schools and hidden command centers in orchards for our headquarters—which were not hit. But the accuracy and lethality of those attacks left an indelible impression on those Iraqi soldiers who either observed them directly or saw the damage afterwards.

> Commanding general
> Al Nida Republican Guard Division

We never really found any cohesive unit, of any brigade, of any Republican Guard Division.

COL William Grimsley
1st Brigade commander, 3d Infantry Division

The most striking feature of the air campaign was the very high degree of precision attained. The results, compared with those achieved in previous air campaigns, appeared sensational.

John Keegan, 2004

I am a determined nonpartisan former public official who loyally served the past two Administrations. My criticism of the brilliantly executed air-land-sea campaign to disarm Iraq was limited to the "rolling start." My anxieties are, of course, being rapidly washed away by the superb success of our fighting forces—and by the rapid reinforcement of the courageous initial assault elements in accordance with this very daring and successful plan.

GEN Barry R. McCaffrey, USA, retired, 2003

They knew that the only chance they had was to wage a struggle against us that marginalized our air power.

John Pike, 2006

TECHNOLOGY

Technology

Impact

Victory smiles upon those who anticipate the changes in the character of war, not upon those who wait to adapt themselves after the changes occur.

Giulio Douhet

Airpower has been transformed (rather than revolutionized) since Vietnam; and even if it cannot carry the day alone, we would be derelict in our duty as citizens not to consider the possibility of increasing [the] use of airpower as the supported force and ground and sea power as the supporting forces.

Dr. David R. Mets

It may be said that warfare has acquired a new phase—technological war. In the past, research and development were only preparation for the final and decisive testing of new systems in battle. Today the kind and quality of systems which a nation develops can decide the battle in advance and make the final conflict a mere formality—or can bypass conflict altogether.

Gen Bernard Schriever

We should base our security upon military formations which make maximum use of science and technology in order to minimize numbers of men.

Dwight D. Eisenhower

Performance means initiative—the most valuable moral and practical asset in any form of war.

William Sholto Douglas
Marshal of the RAF

New conditions require, for solution—and new weapons require, for maximum application—new and imaginative methods. Wars are never won in the past.

Douglas MacArthur

An air force is always verging on obsolescence and, in time of peace, its size and replacement rate will always be inadequate to meet the full demands of war. Military air power should, therefore, be measured to a large extent by the ability of the existing air force to absorb in time of emergency the increase required by war together with new ideas and techniques.

Hap Arnold

Obsolete weapons do not deter.

Margaret Thatcher

In many instances the information displayed for the commander, when traced back to its origins, rests upon an assumption, an estimate, or an extrapolation of data derived from a field trial of some weapon or item of equipment. Commanders, who have seldom participated in deriving the algorithms by which the information on display before them was drawn, tend to accept the given data as reliable fact, especially when the data are presented in numerical form. These soft links in the chain of remote inputs are fatally easy to overlook.

I. B. Holley Jr.

Some airpower missions demand the best technology the nation can produce. The construct that produced airpower . . . for the Vietnam War came from a conscious decision, in pursuit of cost-effectiveness, to build a force with capabilities only incrementally better than the [adversary's]. Consequently, the US Air Force alone lost 16 wings of aircraft in those eight years.

Gen Larry D. Welch, USAF, retired, 1997

Effects of Introducing Technology

Out of the 16,000 V-1s launched against England and the Low Countries in 1944–5, nearly 7,000 were to be destroyed by fighters, anti-aircraft guns, or barrage balloons. Yet the first waves suffered only 2 per cent attrition. Within a week, however, near to 50 per cent was being registered. Towards the end of the attacks on England, anti-aircraft batteries were shooting down up to 80 per cent of those V-1s that crossed their sights.

Neville Brown

We must be prepared to change requirements and operating procedures to agree with commercial practice if we are to make efficient use of commercial technology. In the fields of space, communications, and information, the time from concept to deployment must be no longer than two years.

USAF Scientific Advisory Board, 1996

The way US military leaders regard technology has changed profoundly over the last 20 years. During the Cold War the United States developed the concept of the reconnaissance strike force, key to its "offset strategy": a combination of stealth aircraft, precision-guided munitions, and advanced surveillance technology to offset superior numbers of Soviet forces. Some military leaders and outside experts believed that such advanced technology was too delicate or would not work in the fog of war. But the concept proved itself in Desert Storm, crushing the Iraqi military force with very low US losses.

SecDef William J. Perry, 1996

In military systems, the second step in the development of a radically new concept must be determined after operational deployment. The warfighters will use the system in innovative ways not described in the manuals, and it is this experience that will define the path to revolution.

USAF Scientific Advisory Board, 1996

We must be prepared for a failure rate greater than 50 percent. Most revolutionary ideas will be opposed by a majority of decision makers.

USAF Scientific Advisory Board, 1996

Intelligence, Surveillance, and Reconnaissance

There will be sensors functioning coopera-
tively aboard small, distributed satellite con-
stellations, sensors aboard uninhabited reconnaissance aerial vehicles (URAVs), sensors
aboard weapons, and sensors on the ground
delivered by URAVs.

USAF Scientific Advisory Board, 1996

The whole art of war consists in getting at
what is on the other side of the hill, or, in
other words, in learning what we do not know
from what we do.

Arthur Wellesley, First Duke of Wellington

It's important to reflect that over half of our
sensors that provide us information about
the battlefield are sensors that ride on air-
breathers, not satellites. And so air dominance for us is absolutely key if we're going
to maintain dominance on the battlefield.

GEN John Shalikashvili, 1997

Think about where you live at home and then
think of a place 125 miles from that location.
If you were to move out of your driveway and
we were orbiting 125 miles away, we would
see you move.

Maj Thomas Grabowski, crewmember, 2006
Joint Surveillance Target Attack Radar System

In the realm of [intelligence, surveillance, and reconnaissance], Allied Force witnessed the first large-scale use of unmanned aerial vehicles (UAVs) with near realtime sensors, which provided persistent surveillance in defended areas without putting air crews at risk.

Anthony H. Cordesman, 1999

In an era where, increasingly, military planners speak of conducting "information warfare" against an opponent, the connection between intelligence, sensor suitability, targeting, and combat operations is obvious. No less significant is the importance of bomb damage assessment. Precision weapons, in short, are only as good as the intelligence that governs and guides their use.

Richard Hallion, 1999

The power of the new information systems will lie in their ability to correlate data automatically and rapidly from many sources . . . the accuracy of a single sensor and processor in identifying targets or threats is severely limited. Detection and identification probabilities increase rapidly with sensor diversity and the false alarm probability and error rates decrease correspondingly.

USAF Scientific Advisory Board, 1996

Information

Information warfare will be the most complex type of warfare in the 21st century, and it will decide who will win and who will lose the war.

Chang Mengxiong

To achieve victory in information warfare, the central issue is control of information.

Maj Gen Wang Pufeng
People's Liberation Army (PLA), 1995

You furnish the pictures and I'll furnish the war.

William Randolph Hearst
Letter to Frederic Remington, 1898

Initial insights gained from over a year of research indicate that network-centric forces are more effective. They can do traditional missions more effectively (faster, better, more efficiently) and importantly, they can do different missions. They can accomplish missions thought impossible until very recently.

John Garstka and David Alberts, 2004

Hackers routinely attempt to get into US military systems. During the Gulf War, hackers from Denmark, Moscow, and Iraq tried to penetrate these systems. Our awareness of these attempts does not necessarily prove there were no successes of which we are unaware.

Col James W. McLendon, 1995

Operational-level cyberwar may, then, be that very "acme of skill" which reduces the enemy will without killing. On the other hand, it may also be the abolition of strategy as it attacks the very rationality the enemy requires to decide for war termination.

George J. Stein, 1995

The essence of information is the negation of uncertainties, or negative entropy. Entropy is disorder, thus negative entropy means order. This means that areas with the greatest uncertainties will have the greatest demands for information. Whoever can turn uncertainties into certainties will gain the upper hand under such conditions.

Timothy L. Thomas, paraphrasing Shu Enze

Those who take part in information war are not all soldiers. Anybody who understands computers may become a "fighter" on the network. Think tanks composed of nongovernmental experts may take part in decision-making; rapid mobilization will not just be directed to young people; information-related industries and domains will be the first to be mobilized and enter the war.

Wei Jincheng, summarizing Dr. Shen Weiguang's concept of "take-home war"

Military force has always been based on the main industry of its day.

Maj Gen J. F. C. Fuller, 1932

It seems to me we've got to leap into the thought process . . . of trying to use information warfare itself to be able to make an attack or even a serious illegal probe very unattractive to the potential perpetrator.

Senator Sam Nunn, 1996

The electron, in my judgment, is the ultimate precision guided munition.

John M. Deutch, 1996

The B-2, which is one of the newest aircraft we have, has an avionics suite that is written in Jovial. I programmed in Jovial when I was in the Navy in 1969, and it was kind of a dead language then. It's almost the equivalent of speaking ancient Greek today. It's going to be an industrial base issue, a personnel issue. . . . Even the commercial stuff that's on our aircraft was commercial 15, 20 years ago, and it's no longer actually being maintained.

F. Whitten Peters
Former Secretary of the Air Force, 2001

Technologically, we should try harder to go where others have not trodden and develop uncommon technology. We can also consider organizing some "network special warfare

137

detachments" and finding some computer experts to form a shock brigade of "network warriors" who specialize in looking for critical nodes and control centers on the enemy network and sabotaging them.

Li Yinnian

Thus, as important to modern warfare as information capability has become, it now takes several orders of magnitude [of] improvement to make a significant difference in capability. For example, a system capable of generating imagery accurate to the inch is not necessarily 144 times better than one capable of generating accuracy to the foot, even though the former reveals 144 times as much information, in the technical sense. This is not true for some other aspects of warfare. For example, tank guns that can be aimed accurately from 4,500 meters give overwhelming advantage to an armored force engaging an opponent with tanks armed with guns accurate to only 1,500 meters. In this case, the 3-to-1 superiority alone provides a decisive difference. The performance of Soviet tanks with their Iraqi crews in combat with their American counterparts in the Gulf War made that clear.

Martin C. Libicki, 1996

There may have been a spark of netwar genius in treating the Iraqi soldiers as "brave men put into an impossible situation by a stupid leader." Under such conditions, there is no dishonor in surrendering. And there may have been a glimpse of future netwar—it is rumored that Baghdad Radio signed on one morning with "The Star-Spangled Banner."

George J. Stein, 1995

The Air Force's real strength no longer is the airplanes. The good old days of two incredibly maneuverable planes dogfighting are over and have been overtaken by data links, computers, and satellites.

Richard L. Aboulafia
Aviation analyst, 2005

At present, it appears as though Information Warfare is more of a "bag of tricks" than a system of warfare. As the technologies are better defined, this will change.

USAF Scientific Advisory Board, 1996

Even if two adversaries are generally equal in hard weapons, unless the party with a weaker information capability is able effectively to weaken the information capability of the adversary, it has very little possibility of winning the war. Conversely, if one side can effectively weaken the information capability of the other side, even if its capability in other ways is less, the other side will dare not take any ill-considered action. These two situations constitute "information deterrence." It can prevent war from breaking out. Adroit strategic employment of one's own information deterrence capabilities constitutes an information deterrence strategy.

Chang Mengxiong

Air electronic confrontation equipment, compared to that on the ground, can cover a wider space and have a higher fighting efficiency. The U.S. [armed forces have] developed more than 600 electronic combat devices, of which 70 percent are installed in aircraft.

Maj Gen Zheng Shenxia and
Senior Col Zhang Changzi, PLAAF, 1996

The thrust of China's military construction and development of weapons and equipment will no longer be toward strengthening the "firepower antipersonnel system" of the industrial age, but toward the strengthening of information technology, information weapons systems, and information networking. Our sights must not be fixed on the firepower warfare of the industrial age, rather they must be trained on the information warfare of the information age.

Maj Gen Wang Pufeng, PLA, 1995

Stealth

Surprise was always difficult to achieve because it conflicted with the concepts of mass and concentration. In order to have enough forces available to hurl enough projectiles to win the probability contest, a commander had to assemble and move large numbers. Of course, assembling and moving large forces in secret was quite difficult, cven in the days before aerial reconnaissance, so the odds on surprising the enemy were small indeed. Stealth and precision have solved both sides of the problem; by definition, stealth achieves surprise, and precision means that a single weapon accomplishes what thousands were unlikely to accomplish in the past.

Col John A. Warden III, 1996

Technology

The Emergence of Stealth

I am announcing today a major technological advance of great military significance. This so-called "stealth" technology enables the United States to build manned and un-manned aircraft that cannot be successfully intercepted with existing air defense systems.

This achievement will be a formidable instrument of peace. It promises to add a unique dimension to our tactical forces and the deterrent strength of our strategic forces.

If you believe that a Soviet capability to shoot down all aerodynamic aircraft of the US is a good thing, then you should be very much against this development. If you believe that a US capability to penetrate Soviet air defenses contributes to deterrence as I do, then you will regard this as an advance in stabilizing the arms competition. There is no doubt that bombers which have a longer reaction time are not the destabilizing component. That's land-based fixed ICBM. . . . The ability to penetrate air defenses is not a first strike capability. The ability to penetrate air defenses is a good retaliatory capability.

SecDef Harold Brown, 22 August 1980

World War II demonstrated the decisive role that airpower can play in military operations. It also demonstrated the potential of radar as a primary means of detecting aircraft and directing fire against them.

Because of these developments and because of the importance we attach to maintaining our air superiority, we have for years been developing what we call "penetration" technology: the technology that degrades the effectiveness of radars and other sensors that are used by air defense systems. A particular emphasis has been placed on developing that technology which makes an aircraft "invisible" to radar.

Recognizing the great significance of such a development, we took three related actions: first of all, we made a ten-fold increase in the investment which we are making in this penetration technology, the underlying technology which allows us to defeat the radar systems. Secondly, we initiated a number of very high priority development programs with a purpose of applying this technology; and finally we gave the entire program extraordinary security protection, even to the point of classifying the very existence of the program.

Stealth technology does not involve a single technical approach, a single gimmick so to speak, but is rather a complex synthesis of many. Even if I were willing to describe to you how we do this, I could not do it in a sentence or even in a paragraph.

I do want to emphasize the point, though, that the term invisible is strictly a figure of speech. It is not an invisible airplane. In the strict sense of the word it is not invisible. You can see it. And it is also not invisible to radar. It can be seen by radars if you get the airplane close enough to radars.

Undersecretary of Defense William J. Perry
22 August 1980

Because of his work during the Carter Administration, Dr. Perry is known as the "Father of Stealth." If that's true, it's my job to make sure he keeps up his child-support payments.

Gen Merrill A. McPeak, 1994

The following are some of the critical technical problems that will have to be resolved in China's research on stealth weaponry:

- Expand the stealth waveband. Stealth technology is an important component of electronic warfare, and development of stealth technology must be conducted with full consideration for the peculiarities of modern warfare. The main emphasis on research of stealth weaponry in the various countries is currently placed on centrimetric wave, submillimeter wave, infrared, laser, and metric waveband expansion. The stealth waveband will therefore have to be expanded.

- Meticulous design of the external contours of stealth weaponry. It necessitates streamlining of the exterior of stealth weaponry, eliminating angular reflections and mirror reflections, and the rational design of the exhaust and air intake system of the power unit, to provide minimal surface area for radar reflection.

- Use of the most modern types of radar wave absorption and permeable materials. Exterior coating of the stealth weaponry with wave absorptive material and the use in structural components of wave absorptive and permeable materials can effectively reduce the surface area for radar reflection.

- Selection of power units with limited heat radiation, combined with the cooling of the exhaust fumes will reduce infrared and heat radiation of stealth weaponry and will make it infrared indiscernible.

- Use of electronic countermeasures and increasing the outer impedance load of the stealth weaponry. Installing on stealth weaponry electronic interference mechanisms and various kinds of equipment that would signal out false targets.

- Developing and installing accurate measuring devices. We should place main emphasis on setting up radar testing plants that are consonant with the environment of modern warfare, develop newly structured radar, taking as our principal research objective measurement of the reflecting surface area of the radar targets under wideband conditions, and should thoroughly research the reaction in the targets of the radar waves.

Cao Benyi, 1992

Precision

The precision weapon exemplifies the principle of the low-cost threat that forces a high-cost and complicated defense.

Richard Hallion, 1999

Above all, PGMs connect political objectives to military execution with much greater reliability than ever before. The political leader can have far greater confidence that discrete objectives can be met and can thus gain broader latitude in formulating the overall objective. This is not just a change in air power or even in military power; it is a fundamental change in warfare.

Lt Gen Charles G. Boyd, 1991

Any air force can launch occasional raids or surges of force against a few targets. With adequate preparation, as in the case of the Iraqi raids on Larak Island in 1986 and 1987 during the Iran-Iraq war, such raids can be quite spectacular, and may exercise a temporarily dazzling psychological effect, or even a momentary operational effect (for example, by closing straits to maritime traffic).

Eliot A. Cohen, 1995

The Iraqi Air Force employed PGMs as preferred weapons on targets such as bridges, air defense sites, oil tankers, nuclear plants,

oil storage facilities, and satellite downlinks.
The Iraqi Air Force raid on Larak Island on 25
May 1988 was particularly spectacular; it sank
the world's largest ship, the Seawise Giant,
and three other oil tankers.

The era of smart weapons is here. Yet we do
not seem to be as smart as our weapons.

William M. Arkin, 2000

The tremendous military value of weapons
that can be employed with very high confidence in their outcome creates a demand for
corresponding insight in the fields of intelligence preparation and operational planning.

Gen Ronald R. Fogleman

Given the nature of precision weapon warfare, education of decision-makers as to
their capabilities and limitations is critically
important.

Richard Hallion, 1999

A President who understands that capability
has a very powerful tool, because he has reduced the extent to which his policy is now hos-
tage to the errant bomb or the errant missile.

Maj Gen Chuck Link

As weapons increase in lethality, precision and standoff, intercepting any hostile platform early in its flight is increasingly important.

Gen Ronald R. Fogleman

But the accuracy standard applied by the military is so extraordinarily strict that civilians are seldom put at risk, assuming that the target was properly selected in the first place. An aimpoint might be, for instance, the center of Hall Three of the Lola Utva factory. If the weapon lands 500 feet away on Hall One, it is said to be a miss.

In most cases, the level of accuracy is so much greater today than ever before that a "miss" hardly ever means that civilians will be harmed. But that is not the way the public, the press, or even military spokespersons seem to understand it. To the public and the press, a "miss" strongly suggests an unfortunate and brutally bad outcome. To the military, a miss simply means failure. Neither assumption is necessarily true.

William M. Arkin, 2000

Surgical air strikes are a growing aspect of air power employment in high-tech local wars. [Their] strategic objective is obtained by precisely attacking the enemy's sensitive strategic targets.

Col Ming Zengfu, PLAAF, 1995

Unmanned Aerial Vehicles

The secret of future air power lies in wireless control, that is, in electrical science. The air must wed the ether if air power is to dominate in war; and when this union is consummated, as I will show, the offensive may become so powerful and so difficult to counter, that ultimately nations may decide that the game of war is not worth the candle.

Maj Gen J. F. C. Fuller, 1932

UAVs enjoy the enormous advantage over space-based optical sensors of being able to operate under cloud cover. Given their special capabilities, UAV sensors can identify an object, when sensors on a satellite can only spot it. However, UAVs have great disadvantages. Because they violate airspace, they can create political problems when flown in other than wartime circumstances. UAVs are manpower intensive to operate. . . . Unlike stealth aircraft, UAVs are useless if not communicating.

Martin C. Libicki, 1996

The Army and Marines have an insatiable appetite for full-motion video the Predator supplies. Currently, there is a daily request for more than 300 hours of video a day, and we can only provide about 110 hours.

Lt Col M. E. Bannon, 2005

While the UCAV [unmanned combat air vehicle] has been proposed as a defacto replacement for manned aircraft, we have yet to see the development of artificial intelligence techniques capable of providing UCAVs with more intelligence than that of an insect. Until this software problem is solved, compute cycles will not confer the sought capabilities, especially flexibility, which we find in crewed platforms.

Carlo Kopp, 2002

By far the most significant aspect of the Air war in Afghanistan relates to large-scale employment of Unmanned Aerial Vehicles (UAVs) and Remotely Piloted Vehicles (RPVs) by the coalition forces, specifically the Americans. The Americans, having deployed their Predator UAVs at a secure location in Central Pakistan, were able to undertake a virtual round-the-clock surveillance of the entire area of interest in Afghanistan. The information being acquired by the Predator UAVs was transmitted in real-time through a data down-link which allowed almost simultaneous vectoring of USAF offensive assets which were already airborne, onto the selected target.

Air Commodore Tariq Mahmud Ashraf
Pakistan air force

Technology

Synergies

Progress in a particular direction, aircraft speed or whatever, is usually registered via a diversity of increments (more exotic fuel, innovations in engine design, improved wings and so on). Nonetheless, the cumulative result is likely to approximate a sigmoid curve [of sudden acceleration and deceleration].

Neville Brown

The addition of new armament, command and control, and intelligence technologies to matured aviation technology resulted in a combination that yielded a great improvement in the cost-effectiveness of the aerial offensive—notwithstanding the maturation of air defense systems during the same period. The combination produced a synergy that changed the calculus of conventional war; and it was demonstrated in the Israeli operations in the Bekáa Valley, the Persian Gulf War, and the air war over Serbia. Enthusiasts called it an RMA [revolution in military affairs], others called it a transformation, and still others called it a pipe dream.

Dr. David R. Mets

From the time of the Crimean War a century and a half ago until recently, platforms were militarily crucial: the newest ship, plane, or tank. Now what the platform carries—sensors, munitions, and electronics—matters more than the platform itself.

Mortimer B. Zuckerman, 1997

We have a lot of capabilities that can be glued together quickly to create a new military capability.

Stephen Younger, director
Defense Threat Reduction Agency, 2004

The future force will become efficient and effective through the use of information systems to enhance US operations and to confound the enemy. The infancy of this capability is represented today in the F-22. Information and Space will become inextricably entwined. The Information/Space milieu will interact strongly with the air and ground components, and it is here that commercial technologies and systems will have the largest presence. Defense will not be a driver of important technologies in this area.

USAF Scientific Advisory Board, 1996

The linkage of advanced sensors, advanced precision weapons (particularly smaller ones), long-range combat aircraft, stealth, information technologies, and the ability to strike multiple aimpoints virtually simultaneously, offers the best hope for militarily confronting the variety of challenges we will face, particularly the proliferation of weapons of mass destruction by rogue nations.

Dr. Richard P. Hallion, 1999

Technology and Numbers

We have never been likely to get into trouble by having an extra thousand or two of up-to-date airplanes at our disposal. As the man whose mother-in-law had died in Brazil replied, when asked how the remains should be disposed of, "Embalm, cremate, and bury. Take no risks."

Winston Churchill, April 1938

One can never have too many guns; one never has enough.

Napoléon

The burning wreck of one aircraft or one white parachute spilling out against the sky [was] often glimpsed by many pilots when they twisted and turned five miles high. There can be no doubt that in the confused and intricate air fighting, many of our claims were duplicated, but, wisely, those in authority were not concerned with mere numbers, but with the greater issues of whether or not the Luftwaffe was being held at bay.

Johnnie Johnson

The hope of the wisdom essential to the general direction of men's affairs lies not so much in wealth of specialized knowledge as in the habits and skills required to handle problems involving very diverse viewpoints which must be related to new concrete situations. Wisdom is based on broad understanding in perspective. It is never the product of scientific, technological, or other specializations, though men so trained may, of course, acquire it.

Wallace B. Donham

It is true that [in Germany in World War II] unheard-of inventions and progress were made in individual fields, far ahead of the rest of the world, but they all came too late and . . . they came in such small numbers that they could no longer be decisive.

Karl Koller

Technology

Reactions to Technology

No form of transportation ever really dies out. Every new form is an addition to, and not a substitution for, an old form of transportation.

Air Marshal Trenchard

When offensive weapons make a sudden advance in efficiency, the reaction of the side which has none is to disperse, to thin out, to fall back on medieval guerrilla tactics which would appear childish if they did not rapidly prove to have excellent results.

Gen G. J. M. Chassin

The highly sophisticated industrial economy of the advanced nations of the world, the degree of urbanization of their demographic distribution, and the high standard of living, make them very sensitive to weapons of mass annihilation and area destruction. On the other hand, the underdeveloped areas of the world display a hardening of conflict when faced with such weapons and resort to guerrilla warfare, where man is superior to machine. . . . People used to high material standards of living are most unlikely to harden their will in the face of mass annihilation and area destruction and resort to guerrilla warfare.

S. T. Das

The scientific and technical talents of the contemporary world are spread rather evenly among all potential contenders. This means that whoever invents whatever new device to supplement his power, the other will not be long in shaping it himself for his own uses. While he is doing it, his primary interest will be not in bringing the device to maximum effectiveness, but in the study of it for deficiencies.

J. M. Cameron

It requires more aircraft to transport a light infantry division than to move the total number of PGMs delivered during the Gulf War. . . . What moves into a theater—and when—should be determined by its ability to effectively influence an adversary.

Brig Gen David A. Deptula, 2001

Our damage assessment once again contradicted the conventional wisdom that bombing is, by its nature, indiscriminate and immoral. But the design of the air campaign also offered little comfort to air power zealots, who often argue that air warriors, especially in the United States, have it all figured out—that they know just what to do with their smart weapons.

William M. Arkin, 2000

Best of all, no nation on Earth can assemble a system to match us. And therein lies the problem. Since they can't, they probably won't bother to try. What they will do is use bits and snippets of new technology—begged, borrowed, purchased or stolen—to bypass, degrade, and perhaps destroy an RMA force . . . or perhaps blackmail or intimidate us into not acting at all.

Philip Gold, 1997

PRINCIPLES OF WAR

Principles
of War

Principles
of War

Foundation

The principles of war provide a common un-derstanding across the armed forces. Airmen may find them invaluable in understanding how soldiers think.

Principles of War are only the principles of common sense applied to war.

J. C. Slessor
Lecture to Air War College, 1957

The ideas about strategy which have evolved from time to time no sooner gained acceptance than they were stripped to their barest essen-tials and converted into maxims or, as they have latterly come to be called, "principles." The baggage that was stripped normally con-tained the justifications, the qualifications, and the instances of historical application or misapplication.

Bernard Brodie

Principles of war, though they can be simply stated, are not easy to learn, and can never be learned from books alone. They are the principles of human nature; and whoever learned from books how to deal successfully with his fellows? War which drives human nature to its last resources is a great engine of education, teaching no lessons which it does not illustrate, and enforcing all its lessons by bitter penalties.

Walter Raleigh
War in the Air

The primary elements of tactics are to be seen in their simplest form in a fight between two unarmed men. They are: to think, to guard, to move, and to hit.

J. F. C. Fuller

For they had found that true safety was to be found in long previous training, not in eloquent exhortations uttered when they were going into action.

Thucydides

Those who expect to reap the blessings of freedom must like men, undergo the fatigue of supporting it.

Thomas Paine

In war, the moral is to the physical as three is to one.

Napoléon

It should be remembered that the statements of the *Principles of War* were derived from study of surface operations and written by soldiers with ground warfare in mind. They stem from periods of history when the airplane existed only in the minds of men.

Nathan F. Twining
Quoting a 1947 Air War College seminar

Objective

Compare to the topic of "Effects" under the "War" section (pp. 72–75).

The single path to success in aerial warfare is unwavering adherence to the Principle of the Objective. The adaptability of air forces to many missions and the ease with which they may be diverted encourage vacillation and defeat.

"General Air Force Principles"
Lecture, Air Corps Tactical School, 1934–35

The ordinary man is much more likely to do the right thing if he really understands why he is doing it, and what will probably happen if he does something else; and the best basis for sound judgment is a knowledge of what has been done in the past, and with what results.

J. C. Slessor

General MacArthur approved [my] program and said to go ahead, that I had carte blanche to do anything that I wanted to do. He said he didn't care how my gang was handled, how they looked, how they dressed, how they behaved, or what they did, so long as they would fight, shoot down [Japanese airplanes], and put bombs on the target.

Gen George Kenney

The mission of tactical fighter and fighter-bomber units is to engage in operational missions, as directed by higher echelons within the theater air structure. These operations may be independent of or in conjunction with surface action, but in any event are all directed toward the effective, efficient, and economical accomplishment of the theater commander's assigned mission.

AFM 51-44, *Fighter and Fighter-Bomber Employment in Tactical Air Operations*, 1953

There were two extremely important points about him [Yamamoto] as a commander. First, he made the objectives of the operation extremely clear, and he expressed them with indomitable will. Second, although he did not permit any criticism of the objectives of the operation, he entrusted the details of its execution to the discretion of his subordinates.

Lt Gen Minoru Genda

Successful operations depend on the entire wing organization working as a team with but one purpose in mind. The purpose, of course, is to make certain of the destruction of the selected target at exactly the right time and place. All of the years of planning and training, and the great financial and personal costs and sacrifice, will be vindicated by the successful execution of the mission; likewise,

Principles of War

166

all will be wasted by failure, regardless of its cause.

AFM 51-44, *Fighter and Fighter-Bomber Employment in Tactical Air Operations*, 1953

An irresolute general who acts without principles and without plan, even though he lead an army numerically superior to that of the enemy, almost always finds himself inferior to the latter on the field of battle. Fumblings, the middle course, lose all in war.

Napoléon

> At the same time, the nature of the enemy and the immediate threat he poses to national and friendly forces, demand action that may distract full commitment to one's own objectives.
>
> S. T. Das

Unity of Command

One of the outstanding characteristics of air-power proved to be its flexibility and the terrific concentration made possible by a unified air command—a unity only achieved by a faith born of mutual under-standing between all branches and ranks of the air forces.

Lord Tedder

There is a weakness in a council running a war. That is true of any council. I don't care if it is composed of the best men in the world. . . . In war, you must have decision. A bum decision is better than none. And the trouble is that when you get three, you finally get none.

Dwight Eisenhower

Principles
of War

The compromise which forms the mean be-tween several plans usually combines their faults rather than their merits.

Sir Charles Oman

Nothing is more important in war than unity in command.

Napoléon

My observation is [that] where one person is found adequate to the discharge of a duty by close application, it is worse executed by two and scarcely done at all by three.

Friedrich von Steuben

The same consequences which have uniformly attended long discussions and councils of war will follow at all times. They will end in adoption of the worst course, which in war is always the most timid, or, if you will, the most prudent. The only true wisdom in a general is determined courage.

Napoléon

An educated guess is just as accurate and far faster than compiled errors.

George Patton

Unity of command is not alone sufficient. Unity of planning, unity of common item procurement, and unity of doctrine are equally necessary.

Hap Arnold

Principles
of War

We are seemingly still in the period of transition Douhet described in 1928. . . . He said then that there were men competent to wage war on land, others to wage war at sea, and still others to wage war in the air, but that there were not yet men competent to wage war in general.

Louis A. Sigaud, 1941

Offensive, Initiative, and Surprise

The power of the initiative might be related to the principle of surprise. Without initiative, the best one can do is to hold one's own. With the power of the initiative, the opposition can be destroyed. It would therefore seem axiomatic that the first principle of our national security policy would be to seize and maintain the initiative in all dimensions of modern war; to include the economic, psychological, political, military, and the technological.

Nathan Twining

Offense is the essence of air power.

Hap Arnold

Your first priority is to take the offensive.

Lt Gen Jimmy Doolittle, 1944

Don't hit at all if it is honorably possible to avoid hitting; but never hit soft [*sic*].

Theodore Roosevelt

True offensive doctrine consists of creating favorable situations when they do not otherwise exist, striking at the enemy with the maximum power at the decisive time and place, and driving home the effort determinedly until the desired results have been accomplished.

AFM 51-44, *Fighter and Fighter-Bomber Employment in Tactical Air Operations*, 1953

The offensive knows what it wants, whereas the defensive is in a state of uncertainty.

S. T. Das, paraphrasing Moltke, the Elder

In order to have rest oneself it is necessary to keep the enemy occupied.

Frederick the Great

It is much better to go over difficult ground where you are not expected than it is over good ground where you are expected.

George Patton

Air forces characteristically take the offensive. Even in defense, they defeat an invading enemy by attack.

AU Manual 1, *United States Air Force Basic Doctrine*, 1951

Success is to be obtained only by simultaneous efforts, directed upon a given point, sustained with constancy, and executed with decision.

Archduke Charles of Austria

An air force commander must exploit the extreme flexibility, the high tactical mobility, and the supreme offensive quality inherent in air forces, to mystify and mislead his enemy, and so to threaten his various vital centers as to compel him to be dangerously weak at the point which is really decisive at the time.

J. C. Slessor

The Offensive Aim

To strike with strong effect, one must strike at weakness.

B. H. Liddell Hart

In place of hitting at a *vital* spot, however tough, they committed the deadly tactical sin of looking for a soft spot.

J. F. C. Fuller, describing a World War I battle

Hold out baits to entice the enemy. . . . Amid the turmoil and tumult of battle, there may be seeming disorder and yet no disorder at all; amid confusion and chaos, your array may be without head or tail, yet it will be proof against defeat.

Simulated disorder postulates perfect discipline; simulated fear postulates courage; simulated weakness postulates strength.

Sun Tzu

The Defender's Dilemma

The spot where we intend to fight must not be made known; for then the enemy will have to prepare against a possible attack at several different points; and his forces being thus distributed in many different directions, the numbers we shall have to face at any given point will be proportionately few.

Sun Tzu

Petty geniuses attempt to hold everything; wise men hold fast to the key points. They parry great blows and scorn little accidents. There is an ancient apothegm: he who would preserve everything, preserves nothing. Therefore, always sacrifice the bagatelle and pursue the essential.

Frederick the Great

[The French army in Vietnam] suffers from the considerable disadvantage attaching to those who seek to protect and preserve rather than simply destroy. It is much easier to cut a railway line or blow up a bridge than to protect them from destruction.

Gen G. J. M. Chassin, 1952

The general is skillful in attack whose opponent does not know what to defend; and he is skillful in defense whose opponent does not know what to attack.

Sun Tzu

Limits of the Offensive

It is dangerous to make a fetish of any principle or to become the slave of any tactical doctrine as the French did in 1914. Just as it may sometimes be necessary to divert temporarily even the whole of our air forces to the *strategically* defensive role for reasons of security, so on occasions we may be compelled for the same reason to divert part of our fighter strength to the tactical defensive.

J. C. Slessor, 1936

Military organizations generally prefer offensive doctrines because they reduce uncertainty and enhance military autonomy and resources. But . . . because military organizations seek autonomy, their offensive doctrines are usually poorly integrated with the political aspects of grand strategy.

Daniel J. Hughes

The sands of history are littered with the wrecks of States which set their compass on an offensive course only.

S. T. Das

Using the Initiative: Agitation

Offensive action has often been used to provoke reactions, to force an opponent to make mistakes. Just as certainly, one's enemies are likely to try probing and stirring in return.

Agitate the enemy and ascertain the pattern of his movement. Determine his dispositions and so ascertain the field of battle. Probe him and learn where his strength is abundant and where deficient.

Sun Tzu

Attacks on the decision element of command are limited only by the imagination. They can range from direct strikes at enemy command posts to complex operations to mislead the enemy and induce him to do something inappropriate.

Col John A. Warden III
The Air Campaign

I started shooting when I was much too far away. That was merely a trick of mine. I did not mean so much to hit him as to frighten him, and I succeeded in catching him. He began flying in curves and this enabled me to draw near.

Baron Manfred von Richthofen

Using the Initiative: Alternatives

Maintaining sensible alternatives is like taking a good stance in sports; the purpose is to preserve the benefits of the initiative.

If the enemy is certain as to your point of aim he has the best possible chance of guarding himself—and blunting your weapon. If, on

the other hand, you take a line that threat-
ens alternative objectives, you distract his
mind and forces.

B. H. Liddell Hart

The question "Where should the decisive
point be sought?" does not arise; the question is, "How can a preponderance of force be
brought against the enemy's will?"

There are two answers to this question: to
do something which the enemy cannot prevent, and to do something which he does not
suspect.

J. F. C. Fuller

The Offensive Spirit

No guts, no glory. If you are going to shoot
him down, you have to get in there and mix it
up with him.

Col Frederick C. "Boots" Blesse

I always thought to go around in circles,
slower and slower, was a ridiculous thing. . . .
It's not the way to fight. The best tactic is to
make a pass, then break off and come back.
If you don't do this you'll lose people. One
can't be greedy.

Brig Gen Robin Olds

Find the enemy and shoot him down; anything else is nonsense.

Baron Manfred von Richthofen

When we study the lives of the great captains, and not merely their victories and defeats, what do we discover? That the mainspring within them was *originality*, outwardly expressing itself in unexpected actions.

J. F. C. Fuller

Originality is the most vital of all military virtues as two thousand years of history attest.

In peace it is at a discount, for it causes the disturbance of comfortable ways without producing dividends, as in civil life. But in war, originality bears a higher premium than it can ever do in a civil profession.

B. H. Liddell Hart

Never forget that no military leader has ever become great without audacity.

Clausewitz

An aggressive act in the initial phases of the attack will very often give you a breather and a head start home. . . . Showing a willingness to fight often discourages the enemy even when he outnumbers us, while on the other hand I have, by immediately breaking for the deck on other occasions, given the enemy a "shot in the arm," turning his half-hearted attack into an aggressive one.

Gen John C. Meyer

Principles of War

Mass, Concentration, and Economy of Force

The alternative to massing forces is piecemeal employment—a practice summarized by the phrase "defeat in detail."

We had been taught a lesson, brutally and unmistakably. The first round in modern war takes place in the air—the fight for air superiority; and to be successful one must have reasonable strength in quantity as well as quality, and one's air bases must have security—the security given by warning systems, by dispersal, by protection and by guns. In Greece and Crete we had none of these things. The lesson is clear. It was no use having a victorious and predominant surface fleet if it was not free to operate because we had lost control of the air; it was no use having a strong army if, for the same reason, it could not be supplied and maintained.

Lord Tedder

The principles of Mass were better stated: "Mass is the concentration of *optimum* combat power selected from the available maximum, to be used at a critical time and place."

J. M. Cameron

The principles of war could, for brevity, be condensed into a single word: concentration.

B. H. Liddell Hart

Whereas to shift the weight of effort on the ground from one point to another takes time, the flexibility inherent in Air Forces permits them without change of base to be switched from one objective to another in the theatre of operations. So long as this is realised then the whole weight of the available air power can be used in selected areas in turn. This concentrated use of the air striking force is a battle winning factor of the first importance. It follows that control of the available air power must be centralised and command must be exercised through Air Force channels. Nothing could be more fatal to successful results than to dissipate the air resources into small packets placed under command of land formation commanders, with each packet working on its own plan. The soldier must not expect or wish to exercise direct command over air striking forces.

Field Marshal Montgomery

Numerical weakness comes from having to prepare against possible attacks; numerical strength, from compelling our adversary to make these preparations against us.

Sun Tzu

Economy of Force

In the last war, air-power forfeited much of its effect from being kept in separate packets like the parts of an army, with a consequent dispersion of effort and frittering of effect.

B. H. Liddell Hart

The principle of Economy of Force is sometimes misunderstood as holding back a large body of troops and committing the minimum force to battle. This is not the true interpretation or application of the law. To hold back troops when they can be gainfully employed is false economy. The use of reserves on the other hand is a tactical application of the same principle. When information is lacking or the situation is such that only after the initial engagement can the enemy's weak spot be discovered, in such cases reserves are not really held back from the battle but are actually kept ready for battle when the decisive time and place has been reached.

S. T. Das

Economy of Force rightly means, not a mere husbanding of one's resources of manpower, but the employment of one's force, both men and weapons, in accordance with the economic laws, so as to yield the highest possible dividends of success in proportion to strength.

B. H. Liddell Hart

Economy of Force is the supreme law of successful war because in a trial of strength a nation's capacity to stand the strain depends not merely on the extent of its resources, but on their economic distribution.

B. H. Liddell Hart

It was the strategy employed by raiders since naval war began, to strike in one area until the strength of the enemy was directed thither, and then to slip away and start again in a fresh unguarded area.

C. S. Forester
The Age of Fighting Sail

The principles of mobility and concentration of force were considered to be contradictory elements of principles of war till the arrival of airpower. Today the exponents of airpower maintain that the principles of offensive and economy of force can be achieved effectively only by the exploitation of airspace, whereas prior to the emergence of airpower the principle of offensive could only be applied by maintaining a 4-to-1 ratio over the enemy forces.

S. T. Das

There are generally insufficient forces to conduct extensive operations in all air tasks at one time; thus the selection of targets and the allocation of effort must be in terms of the needs of the theater. Enemy action may necessitate a major revision in task priorities.

AFM 1-3, *Theater Air Operations*, 1953

To me an unnecessary action, or shot, or casualty, was not only waste but sin.

T. E. Lawrence

Maneuver and Mobility

The enemy must not know where I intend to
give battle. For if he does not know where I
intend to give battle, he must prepare in a
great many places. . . . For if he prepares to
the front his rear will be weak, and if to the
rear, his front will be fragile. If he prepares to
the left his right will be vulnerable and if to
the right, there will be few on the left. And
when he prepares everywhere he will be weak
everywhere.

Sun Tzu

I believe that, more or less, all of the Allied
operations [in the Southwest Pacific] de-
pended on deception by landing in places
where we thought a landing and the building
of airfields impossible.

Lt Col Masaru Shinohara
Japanese Eighth Area Army

Modern war is a war for airbases; the bull-
dozer must accompany the plane. . . . One of
the elements of victory in North Africa was
the speed with which our aviation engineers
constructed airfields behind the front lines
and pressed the attack.

Hap Arnold

Maximum time over target or extreme depth
of penetration may be necessary. This nor-

mally requires that aircraft be based as close to the target areas as possible. Since ground action is often fluid in nature, tactical air units must possess a considerable degree of mobility. It is essential that all components of the tactical air organization, including supporting or service units, be able to move from site to site without disrupting the combat mission. Equipment should be designed with this in mind and, whenever possible, be air transportable.

AFM 51-44, *Fighter and Fighter-Bomber Employment in Tactical Air Operations*, 1953

The giant airbases of today will become the bomber cemeteries of a future war.

Gen P. F. Zhigarev
Soviet air forces, 1958

The strength of air forces lies in mobility and flexibility. These characteristics permit concentration of massed firepower at the place and time dictated by the situation with maximum surprise. Mobility and flexibility are reduced when:

a. Air forces are compartmented in separate units under separate commands, and
b. Are allotted to lower echelons.

AU Manual 1, *United States Air Force Basic Doctrine*, 1951

Simplicity

Remember, gentlemen, an order that can be misunderstood will be misunderstood.

Moltke, the Elder

The ability to distinguish essentials from non-essentials, to grasp quickly the elements of the changing situation, and the intestinal fortitude to keep cool and to continue fighting when the going gets tough are required in the successful war commander.

Adm Raymond A. Spruance

Difficulties always arise from attempts to improve to the point of achieving what is not possible, thereby failing to gain what is well within reach.

J. M. Cameron

The principal message of fog, friction and chance is that strategy must be flexible. Plans that rely on flawless execution are overly susceptible to failure. Plans that rely on rigid timetables and rigidly sequenced actions are overly susceptible to failure. In general, the more complex the plan, the more likely that something will go awry.

Dennis Drew and Donald Snow

Few orders are best, but they should be followed up with care.

Maurice de Saxe

Security

The whole art of war consists of a well-reasoned and extremely circumspect defensive followed by rapid and audacious attack.

Napoléon

Skepticism is the mother of security. Even though only fools trust their enemies, prudent persons never do. One falls into a feeling of security after battles, when one is drunk with success, and when one believes the enemy completely disheartened. One falls into a feeling of security when a skillful enemy amuses you with pretended peace proposals. One falls into a feeling of security by mental laziness.

Frederick the Great

Always presume that the enemy has dangerous designs and always be forehanded with the remedy. But do not let these calculations make you timid.

Frederick the Great

Three can keep a secret if two of them are dead.

Benjamin Franklin

Our continuous air offensive had evidently annoyed them, as the raid was made by twenty-four bombers escorted by about the same number of fighters. We lost eleven aircraft on the ground at Seven Mile Airdrome. In addition, the operations building was burned down, several trucks destroyed, two hundred drums of gasoline went up in smoke, and the runway was hit in several places. The Japanese left eight calling-cards in the shape of long-delay time-fuzed bombs which exploded at intervals all the way up to forty-four hours. Several men were wounded by bomb fragments. Once again our warning service was inadequate.

Gen George Kenney

Constants—If Not Principles—of War

Communications

If intercommunications between events in front and ideas behind are not maintained, then two battles will be fought—a mythical headquarters battle and an actual front-line one, in which case the real enemy is to be found in our own headquarters.

J. F. C. Fuller

Congress can make a general but only communications can make him a commanding general.

GEN Omar Bradley

Public Support

Except for valid security reasons, any action that cannot be satisfactorily explained to the troops, the Congress, and the general public, should be regarded as suspect and thoroughly examined.

GEN Matthew B. Ridgway

Integrity is the fundamental premise for military service in a free society. Without integrity, the moral pillars of our military strength, public trust, and self-respect are lost.

Gen Charles A. Gabriel

By rapidity many measures of the enemy are nipped in the bud, and public opinion is gained in our favor.

Clausewitz

It is strange that except by Clausewitz and to some extent by Macklin, the Principle of "Public Opinion" has not been considered very vital even by the modern military theoreticians.

S. T. Das

Logistics

When the enemy assesses our forces, he values only those forces which the logistics community has ready for combat, or can get ready in time, and then sustain for a requisite period of time.

F. M. Rogers

My logisticians are a humorless lot . . . they know if my campaign fails, they are the first ones I will slay.

Alexander the Great

My Dear General, this expanding and piling up of impedimentia [*sic*] has been so far almost our ruin, and will be our final ruin if it is not abandoned.

Abraham Lincoln to Gen Nathaniel P. Banks
on the inability of the Union Army to move
due to logistic excesses

Logistics controls all campaigns and limits many.

Dwight Eisenhower

The crews of a heavy bombardment group in China must ferry over their own gasoline, bombs, replacement parts and everything else in their own B-24s. Before this bombardment group can go on one combat flight, it must make four trips over the Hump. To perform one extremely dangerous mission, those crews must make four separate flights over the most hazardous terrain in the world.

Hap Arnold

What I want to avoid is that my supplies should command me.

Comte de Guibert

Logistics is the bridge between the economy of the nation and the tactical operations of its combat forces. Obviously, then, the logistics system must be in harmony, both with the economic system of the nation and with the tactical concepts and environment of the combat forces.

Adm Henry E. Eccles

The ideal for all military forces is to reduce their logistical requirements to necessities only.

AFM 1-1, *Basic Aerospace Doctrine of the United States Air Force*, 1992

I don't know what the hell this logistics is that Marshall is always talking about, but I want some of it.

Adm E. J. King

Air logistics is defined as that section of military science that embraces the details of planning for, and preparation of, all of the means and facilities required to make a combat force operational and capable of sustaining its action.

Maj Gen Elmer D. Adler

The essence of flexibility is in the mind of the commander, the substance of flexibility is in logistics.

Adm Henry E. Eccles

It is very necessary to attend to all this detail and to trace a biscuit from Lisbon into a man's mouth on the frontier and to provide for its removal from place to place by land or by water, or no military operations can be carried out.

Wellington

We have a claim on the output of the arsenals of London as well of Hanyang, and what is more, it is to be delivered to us by the enemy's own transport corps. This is the sober truth, not a joke.

Mao Tse-tung

The sinews of war are five—men, money, materials, maintenance and morale.

Bernard M. Baruch

When the Duke of Cumberland has weakened his army sufficiently, I shall teach him that a general's first duty is to provide for its welfare.

Maurice de Saxe

I believe that the task of bringing the force to the fighting point, properly equipped and well-formed in all that it needs is at least as important as the capable leading of the force in the fight itself. . . . In fact, it is indispensable, and the combat between hostile forces is more in the preparation than the fight.

Gen Sir John Monash

Mobility is the true test of a supply system.

B. H. Liddell Hart

In my opinion, there is no one single piece of foresightedness that helped our war effort more than the policy that kept our depots intact and operating on an efficient basis.

Maj Gen Oliver P. Echols

Be nice to your mother but love your logisticians and communicators.

Gen Charles A. Horner

Time

During the last great aerial raid on England, the German Air Force flew about 1,200 bombers over industrial targets which were critical to the survival of the British Empire. At the same time the Royal Air Force Fighter Command consisted of little more than a handful of trained pilots and fighter planes. The incredible German decision to stagger the attack, and to use twelve hours for its completion, actually multiplied the strength of the Royal Air Force Fighter Command by a factor of five. This was possible because on that day each Spitfire pilot had the time to fly five missions.

Nathan Twining

When you seem to be most prodigal of the soldier's blood, you spare it, by supporting your attacks well and by pushing them with the greatest vigor to prevent time from augmenting your losses.

Frederick the Great

Quick decisions are unsafe decisions.

Sophocles

The god of war hates those who hesitate.

Euripides

Take time to deliberate, but when the time for action arrives, stop thinking and go on.

Andrew Jackson

Three British Principles

Morale: Success in war depends more on morale than on physical qualities. Numbers, armament, resources or skill can not compensate for lack of courage, energy, determination and the bold offensive spirit which springs from a national determination to conquer.

Flexibility: Modern war demands a high degree of flexibility to enable pre-arranged plans to be altered to meet changing situations and unexpected developments. By strategical and tactical flexibility, force can be concentrated rapidly and economically at decisive places and times. This entails good training, organization, discipline, and staff work, and above all, that rapidity of decision on the part of the commander which ensures that time is never lost.

Administration: The administrative arrangements must be designed to give the commanders the maximum freedom of action in carrying out the plan. Every administrative organization must be simple. Every operational commander must have a degree of control over the administrative plan within his sphere of command, corresponding to the scope of his responsibilities for the operational plan.

> Quoted by Nathan Twining in
> *Neither Liberty nor Safety*

Another Principle: Poise

Air Forces more than surface forces must consciously anticipate, posture, and ready their fighting forces to take advantage of fleeting opportunities. They must be spring loaded without being overcommitted to one anticipated course of events. In the fighter pilot vernacular, command elements must "lead-turn," or constantly stay ahead of, events; they must develop cues to guide increased surveillance and alert status; they must be mentally prepared to herd the enemy rather than simply react. The experience of war indicates that commanders must also economize alertness by aggressively relaxing their forces when opportunities for recovery and rest are achieved. Only ruthless reduction of sensor and information data, to distinguish essentials from all the available information, can permit the mental clarity necessary for optimum poise and perception.

Suggested by the ideas of Clausewitz, *On War*

COMMAND

Command

Human Factors in War

If one could only come to mastery of things inside him, nothing outside could get the better of him.

Col Raynal C. Bolling

With equal or inferior power of destruction he will win who has the resolution to advance, who by his formations and maneuvers can continually threaten his adversary with a new phase of material action, who, in a word, has the moral ascendancy.

Ardant du Picq

Professional Growth

In sum the leader has to achieve a balance between the essential need for professional competence in his own technical field and that broader understanding of human problems which can only be achieved from a wide and largely self-acquired education.

S. W. Roskill

If we wish to think clearly, we must cease imitating; if we wish to cease imitating, we must make use of our imagination. We must train ourselves for the unexpected in place of training others for the cut and dried. Audacity, and not caution, must be our watchword.

J. F. C. Fuller

The essential basis of the military life is the ordered application of force under an unlimited liability. It is the unlimited liability which sets the man who embraces this life somewhat apart. He will be (or should be) always a citizen. So long as he serves he will never be a civilian.

Gen Sir John W. Hackett

A great captain can be formed only by long experience and intense study; neither is his own experience enough—for whose life is there sufficiently fruitful of events to render his knowledge universal?

Archduke Charles of Austria

It is common to see men who have used all their limbs without once in their lives having utilized their minds. Thought, the faculty of combining ideas, is what distinguishes man from a beast of burden. A mule who has carried a pack for ten campaigns under Prince Eugene will be no better a tactician for it, and it must be confessed, to the disgrace of humanity, that many men grow old in an otherwise respectable profession without making any greater progress than this mule.

Frederick the Great

In the profession of war the rules of the art are never violated without drawing punishment from the enemy who is delighted to find us at fault. An officer can spare himself many mistakes by improving himself.

Frederick the Great

Education is a two-edged sword. If it indoctrinates with rigid principles, constantly hammering home the fixed and immutable nature of those principles, and if it offers neat solutions to every human problem in terms of these fixed principles, then change and development can not take place.

Maj Gen Dale 0. Smith

The man who can't make a mistake can't make anything.

Abraham Lincoln

Perhaps the most valuable result of all education is the ability to make yourself do the thing you have to do, when it ought to be done, whether you like it or not.

T. H. Huxley

Few men during their lifetime come anywhere near exhausting the resources dwelling within them. There are deep wells of strength that are never used.

Adm Richard E. Byrd

In battle nothing is ever as good or as bad as the first reports of excited men would have it.

Field Marshal Sir William Slim

One machine can do the work of 50 ordinary men. No machine can do the work of one extraordinary man.

Elbert Hubbard

Of every one hundred men, ten shouldn't even be there. Eighty are nothing but targets, nine are real fighters. . . . We are lucky to have them [for] they make the battle. . . . Ah, but ONE, one of them is a Warrior . . . and he will bring the others back!

Heraclitus ca. 500 BC

Command

The first quality for a commander-in-chief is a cool head, which receives a correct impression of things. He should not allow himself to be confused by either good or bad news. The impressions which he receives successively or simultaneously in the course of a day should classify themselves in his mind in such a way as to occupy the places which they merit, for reason and judgment are the result of comparison of various impressions taken into just consideration.

Napoléon

The qualifications of the combat commander determine to a larger extent than any other single element the effectiveness of a unit in combat.

Hap Arnold

The first requirement to be a military leader is to know thoroughly one's specialty, and the second to be loyal to one's subordinates. Both conditions will save one from mutual disloyalty.

Simón Bolívar

Remember this: the truly great leader overcomes all difficulties, and campaigns and battles are nothing but a long series of difficulties to be overcome. The lack of equipment, the lack of food, the lack of this or that are only excuses; the real leader displays his quality in his triumphs over adversity, however great it may be.

GEN George C. Marshall

I don't mind being called tough, because in this racket it's the tough guys who lead the survivors.

Gen Curtis LeMay

No normal young man is likely to recognize in himself the qualities that will persuade others to follow him. On the other hand, any man who can carry out orders in a cheerful spirit, complete his work step by step, use imagination in improving it, and then when the job is done, can face toward his next duty with anticipation, need have no reason to doubt his own capacity for leadership.

S. L. A. Marshall

I'm firmly convinced that leaders are not born; they're educated, trained, and made, as in every other profession. To ensure a strong, ready Air Force, we must always remain dedicated to this process.

Gen Curtis LeMay

Command

Once you pick up the burden of leadership, you can never put it down again as long as you live. Sergeant or general, we all carry the same load.

GEN Williston B. Palmer

The commander should practice kindness and severity, should appear friendly to the soldiers, speak to them on the march, visit them while they are cooking, ask them if they are well cared for, and alleviate their needs if they have any. Officers without experience in war should be treated kindly. Their good actions should be praised. Small requests should be granted and they should not be treated in an overbearing manner, but severity is maintained about everything regarding duty.

Frederick the Great

I will tell you that a commander without the proper C2 assets commands nothing except a desk.

Gen Ronald R. Fogleman

All a soldier desires to drive him forward is recognition and appreciation of his work.

George Patton

Duty is the sublimest word in our language. Do your duty in all things. You cannot do more. You should never do less.

Robert E. Lee

A hero is no braver than an ordinary man, but he is brave five minutes longer.

Ralph Waldo Emerson

The definition of military training is success in battle. In my opinion that is the only objective of military training.

LtGen Lewis "Chesty" Puller

Advice

Never tell people how to do things. Tell them what to do and they will surprise you with their ingenuity.

George Patton

Every general-in-chief who undertakes to execute a plan that he knows to be bad is culpable. He should communicate his reasons, insist on a change of plan, and finally resign his commission rather than become the instrument of his army's ruin.

Napoléon

When things go wrong in your command, start searching for the reason in increasingly larger concentric circles around your own desk.

GEN Bruce C. Clarke

The principal task of the general is mental, involving large projects and major arrangements. But since the best dispositions become useless if they are not executed, it is essential that the general should be industrious in seeing whether his orders are executed or not.

Frederick the Great

Command

Do what is right, not what you think the higher headquarters wants or what you think will make you look good.

GEN Norman Schwarzkopf

The Commander and the Staff

I had [the general] assemble his whole staff and tried to give them a picture of what we were up against in New Guinea. That was where the war was and it was not moving to Australia. Those youngsters up there were our customers and customers are always right. Our only excuse for living was to help them. We might work ourselves into having stomach ulcers or nervous breakdowns, but those things were not fatal. The work those kids in New Guinea and at Darwin were doing, however, had a high fatality rate. They deserved all they could get. Most of the crowd appreciated what I was talking about. The others would go home.

Gen George Kenney

The staff is simply the servant of the general force; it exists but to further the welfare of the fighting establishment. Those within it are remiss if they fail to keep this rule uppermost.

S. L. A. Marshall

My Lord,

If I attempted to answer the mass of futile correspondence that surrounds me I should be debarred from all serious business of campaigning.

I must remind your Lordship—for the last time—that so long as I retain an independent

Command

position, I shall see to it that no officer under my command is debarred, by mere quill driving in your Lordship's office, from attending to his first duty, which is, and always has been, so to train the private men under his command that they may, without question, best any force opposed to them in the field.

> I am, my Lord
> Your obedient servant,
> Wellington

Possibly apocryphal correspondence, supposedly written in 1810

A bulky staff implies a division of responsibility, slowness of action and indecision, whereas a small staff implies activity and concentration of purpose.

GEN William Tecumseh Sherman

Administration and Combat Support

I must have assistants who will solve their own problems and tell me later what they have done.

GEN George C. Marshall

Nobody in the British Army ever reads a regulation or an order as if it were to be a guide for his conduct, or in any other manner than as an amusing novel; and the consequence is, that when complicated arrangements are to be carried into execution . . . every gentleman proceeds according to his fancy, and then when it is found that the [mission] fails (as it must fail if the order is not strictly obeyed) they come upon me to set matters right and thus my labor is increased tenfold.

Wellington

It is not recognized that the object of regulations and rules is to produce order in the fighting machine, and not to strangle the mind of the man who controls it.

J. F. C. Fuller

There has been a constant struggle on the part of the military element to keep the end—fighting, or readiness to fight—superior to mere administrative considerations. The military man, having to do the fighting, considers that the chief necessity; the administrator equally naturally tends to think the smooth running of the machine the most admirable quality.

Alfred Thayer Mahan

Any commander who fails to exceed his authority is not of much use to his subor-dinates.

Adm Arleigh Burke

Information Management

The central problem is not collecting and transmitting information, but synthesizing for the decision maker.

Richard Burt

There are no "battle management" magic bullets that will substitute for the ability of on-scene commanders, soldiers, and airmen to make appropriate decisions based on the ebb and flow of events.

Richard P. Hallion

To do our work we all have to read a mass of papers. Nearly all of them are far too long. This wastes time, while energy has to be spent in looking for vital points.

I ask my colleagues and their staffs to see to it that their reports are shorter.

The aim should be short reports which set out the main points in a series of short crisp paragraphs. . . .

Let us have an end of such phrases as these: "It is also of importance to bear in mind the following considerations" or "Consideration should be given to the possibility of carrying into effect." Most of these woolly phrases are

Command

mere padding which can be left out altogether, or replaced by a single word.

Let us not shrink from using the short expressive phrase, even if it is conversational.

Reports drawn up on the lines I propose may at first seem rough as compared with the flat officialese jargon. But the saving in time will be great, while the discipline of setting out the real points concisely will prove an aid to clearer thinking.

Winston Churchill, 1940

The main thing is to have a plan; if it is not the best plan, it is at least better than no plan at all.

Gen Sir John Monash

Command

Command Arrangements

It is astonishing how obstinate allies are, how parochially minded, how ridiculously sensitive to prestige and how wrapped up in obsolete political ideas. It is equally astonishing how they fail to see how broad-minded you are, how clear your picture is, how up to date you are and how co-operative and big-hearted you are. It is extraordinary.

Field Marshal Sir William Slim

The proverbial weakness of alliances is due to inferior power of concentration.

Alfred Thayer Mahan

This is notably less of a limitation for combined air forces, which can be concentrated in space and time, can provide simultaneous supporting efforts if differently equipped, can mutually support one another in many ways, and can concentrate over time on particular target systems, objectives, and campaigns.

Of all the lessons we learned about tactical air operations, perhaps the most important is that the air commander, his group and squadron commanders must have a sincere desire to become part of the ground team. The Army must, of course, have the same dedication to reciprocate. This close liaison can come only from close day-to-day contact—especially at command levels; there must be almost instantaneous communication between ground and air and through all the chain of command.

Lt Gen Elwood R. "Pete" Quesada

The greatest lesson of this war has been the extent to which air, land, and sea operations can and must be coordinated by joint planning and unified command. The attainment of better coordination and balance than now exists between services is an essential of national security.

Hap Arnold

It turned out to be another scrambled outfit . . . with so many lines of responsibility, control, and coordination on the chart that it resembled a can of worms as you looked at it. I made a note to tell Walker to take charge, tear up the chart, and have no one issue orders around there except himself. After he got things operating simply, quickly, and efficiently he could draw up a new chart if he wanted to.

Gen George Kenney

Command

Mutual support is the fundamental basis upon which the air-surface relationship is founded.

AFM 1-3, *Theater Air Operations*, 1953

We must not allow Centralized Control–Decentralized Execution to devolve to Centralized Control–Centralized Execution. That construct breeds excessive cautiousness at all levels, stifles initiative, and it is instructive to remember that it was the Soviet command model.

Maj Gen David A. Deptula, 2001

FIELD SERVICE REGULATIONS

COMMAND AND EMPLOYMENT
OF AIR POWER

SECTION I

DOCTRINE OF COMMAND
AND EMPLOYMENT

1. RELATIONSHIP OF FORCES.–LAND POWER AND AIR POWER ARE CO-EQUAL AND INTERDEPENDENT FORCES; NEITHER IS AN AUXILIARY OF THE OTHER.

2. DOCTRINE OF EMPLOYMENT.–THE GAINING OF AIR SUPERIORITY IS THE FIRST REQUIREMENT FOR THE SUCCESS OF ANY MAJOR LAND OPERATION. AIR FORCES MAY BE PROPERLY AND PROFITABLY EMPLOYED AGAINST ENEMY SEA POWER, LAND POWER, AND AIR POWER. HOWEVER, LAND FORCES OPERATING WITHOUT AIR SUPERIORITY MUST TAKE SUCH EXTENSIVE SECURITY MEASURES AGAINST HOSTILE AIR ATTACK THAT THEIR MOBILITY AND ABILITY TO DEFEAT THE ENEMY LAND FORCES ARE GREATLY REDUCED. THEREFORE, AIR FORCES MUST BE EMPLOYED PRIMARILY AGAINST THE ENEMY'S AIR FORCES UNTIL AIR SUPERIORITY IS OBTAINED. IN THIS WAY ONLY CAN DESTRUCTIVE AND DEMORALIZING AIR ATTACKS AGAINST LAND FORCES BE MINIMIZED AND THE INHERENT MOBILITY OF MODERN LAND AND AIR FORCES BE EXPLOITED TO THE FULLEST.

Command

3. COMMAND OF AIR POWER.–THE IN-HERENT FLEXIBILITY OF AIR POWER, IS ITS GREATEST ASSET. THIS FLEXIBILITY MAKES IT POSSIBLE TO EMPLOY THE WHOLE WEIGHT OF THE AVAILABLE AIR POWER AGAINST SELECTED AREAS IN TURN; SUCH CONCENTRATED USE OF THE AIR STRIKING FORCE IS A BATTLE WIN-NING FACTOR OF THE FIRST IMPORTANCE. CONTROL OF AVAILABLE AIR POWER MUST BE CENTRALIZED AND COMMAND MUST BE EXERCISED THROUGH THE AIR FORCE COMMANDER IF THIS INHERENT FLEXIBILITY AND ABILITY TO DELIVER A DECISIVE BLOW ARE TO BE FULLY EX-PLOITED. THEREFORE, THE COMMAND OF AIR AND GROUND FORCES IN A THEATER OF OPERATIONS WILL BE VESTED IN THE SUPERIOR COMMANDER CHARGED WITH THE ACTUAL CONDUCT OF OPERATIONS IN THE THEATER, WHO WILL EXERCISE COMMAND OF AIR FORCES THROUGH THE AIR FORCE COMMANDER AND COM-MAND OF GROUND FORCES THROUGH THE GROUND FORCE COMMANDER. THE SUPERIOR COMMANDER WILL NOT AT-TACH ARMY AIR FORCES TO UNITS OF THE GROUND FORCES UNDER HIS COM-MAND EXCEPT WHEN SUCH GROUND FORCE UNITS ARE OPERATING INDEPEN-DENTLY OR ARE ISOLATED BY DISTANCE OR LACK OF COMMUNICATION.

JULY 1943

DOCTRINE

Doctrine

Basics

Those who are possessed of a definitive body of doctrine and of deeply rooted convictions upon it will be in a much better position to deal with the shifts and surprises of daily affairs than those who are merely taking short views, and indulging their natural impulses as they are evoked by what they read from day to day.

Winston Churchill

If you think education is expensive, try ignorance.

Derek Bok

The organization of men and machines into military forces does not necessarily mean that they are equipped and trained for the accomplishment, if necessary, of decisive action in war. For this, the discipline of a coherent body of thought appears to be indispensable.

Eugene Emme

In short, doctrine is what is officially approved to be taught. But it is far more than just that. Doctrine is the departure for virtually every activity in the air arm.

I. B. Holley Jr.

Doctrine

The way we teach around here nowadays is that doctrine is always wrong. The side that wins is the side whose doctrine is the least wrong and who has a system that is flexible enough to adopt its doctrine once combat reveals the flaws in the doctrine.

Dr. David R. Mets

The standardization of technique of operations is not possible in this global war, for 90 times out of 100 an idea that succeeds in Italy will not work in New Guinea. Hence we must be versatile—our tactics must be susceptible to change—our commanding officers must have ingenuity and imagination.

Hap Arnold

Doctrine is like a compass bearing; it gives us the general direction of our course. We may deviate from that course on occasion, but the heading provides a common purpose to all who travel along the way. This puts a grave burden on those who formulate doctrine, for a small error, even a minute deviation, in our compass bearing upon setting out, may place us many miles away from the target at the end of the flight. If those who distill doctrine from experience or devise it from logical inference in the abstract fail to exercise the utmost rigor in their thinking, the whole service suffers.

I. B. Holley Jr.

Doctrine

There are tens of thousands of individuals in the Air Force whose training and traditions lead them to identify with one or another of the major commands, with SAC [Strategic Air Command] or TAC [Tactical Air Command], or MAC [Military Airlift Command]. And each of these bespeaks a vested interest. Each such interest must be placated, reconciled, accommodated. These necessities, along with the never-ending confrontations with other services fighting for roles and missions, keep the present-day guardians of Air Force doctrine eternally on the run. They are so busy putting out fires, few of them find time in which to think at leisure.

I. B. Holley Jr.

Understanding requires theory; theory requires abstraction; and abstraction requires the simplification and ordering of reality. . . . Obviously, the real world is one of blends, irrationalities, and incongruities: actual personalities, institutions, and beliefs do not fit into neat logical categories. Yet neat logical categories are necessary if man is to think profitably about the real world in which he lives and to derive from it lessons for broader application and use.

Samuel P. Huntington

Doctrine

Example is not the main thing in influencing others. It is the only thing.

Albert Schweitzer

The JFC and JFACC staff should not have to sift through dozens of Joint and service publications to discover how to accomplish assessment. Ultimately, the doctrinal confusion is the fault of Joint doctrine.

Maj Thomas J. Timmerman

Failures in the transmission of information from the desert back to Britain and on to the United States are typical of an ancient theme in military history: the reluctance of tribes, nations, and armed forces to learn except from their own experience.

Vincent Orange

Everyone is equal before truth; earnestly advocate creative and pioneering efforts; let a hundred flowers blossom and a hundred schools of thought contend; and weed through the old to bring forth the new. . . . Draw upon all advanced and beneficial military thinking; make foreign experiences serve China's purposes; and enrich and develop China's military theories.

Gen Fu Quanyou, chief, PLA general staff, 1998

Doctrine

Change and Resistance

Attempting to employ long term fixed doctrine, regulations or legislation to confront changes resulting from evolution is utterly futile. The only thing which will remain fixed is ever increasing change.

Carlo Kopp

The traditions among all the armed services are much older than any government, more conservative than any department of government, and more sure to build on a foundation that they are certain of, rather than to take any chance of making a mistake.

Billy Mitchell

I was to learn later in life that we tend to meet any new situation by re-organizing; and a wonderful method it can be for creating the illusion of progress while producing confusion, inefficiency and demoralization.

Petronius Arbiter ca. 210 BC

The professional soldier is a purely military alchemist; he dabbles in tactical and strategic magic, fashions charms and pentacles, burns incense before training manuals, and when on the battlefield, if he has ever studied military history, conjures forth the ghostly theories of past masters of war in order to solve the problems which there confront him.

Doctrine

The politician is no better, for he knows nothing of war, and yet feels eminently capable to control a War Office or an Admiralty, or even to conduct a campaign. If surgery and medicine were still treated as war is now treated, we should to-day be using grated unicorn's horn and butcher's knives in our hospitals.

J. F. C. Fuller, 1932

Air power speaks a strategic language so new that translation into the hackneyed idiom of the past is impossible.

Alexander de Seversky

The only thing harder than getting a new idea into a military mind is getting an old one out.

B. H. Liddell Hart

There is nothing permanent except change.

Heraclitus, 513 BC

He that will not apply new remedies must expect new evils; for time is the greatest innovator.

Francis Bacon

The intuitive mind is a sacred gift and the rational mind is a faithful servant. We have created a society that honors the servant and has forgotten the gift.

Albert Einstein

Doctrine

A new idea must have three qualities: First, it must have dynamic novelty to spark the imagination; something never tried before. It must overcome the entrenched opposition. Second, it must be feasible of fulfillment, by new means either available or potential. Third, it must promise overwhelming capacity to alter the course of history.

Tooey Spaatz

An army is an institution not merely conservative but retrogressive by nature. It has such natural resistance to progress that it is always insured against the danger of being pushed ahead too fast.

B. H. Liddell Hart

Contrasting Views

Against a lot of solid armies, it's necessary to go forth into death ground at bayonet point and kill the other guy, face to face. . . . The United States continues to trust in airpower and magical technology, then hopes for the best. It may work. But history offers no particular cause for optimism.

COL Daniel P. Bolger, 2003

Cavalry as an assaulting arm proved useless against cavalry, and the bayonet, the weapon of . . . shock, was abruptly dethroned by the bullet [by 1865. The] chief of staff to General J. E. B. Stuart writes "recalling all the battles in which I have borne a part, bayonet-fights rarely if ever occur, and exist only in the imagination."

J. F. C. Fuller, 1932

When, in 1898, I joined the Army, though a normally indifferently educated young Englishman, I was appalled by the ignorance which surrounded me and the immense military value attached to it.

J. F. C. Fuller

A Human Being should be able to change a diaper, plan an invasion, butcher a hog, conn a ship, design a building, write a sonnet, balance accounts, build a wall, set a bone, comfort the dying, take orders, give orders, cooperate, act alone, solve equations, analyze a new problem, pitch manure, program a computer, cook a tasty meal, fight efficiently and die gallantly. Specialization is for insects.

Robert Heinlein

Terminology

The clarity and therefore the utility of doctrine is a direct product of how well language is used in its writing.

How many a dispute could have been deflated into a single paragraph if the disputants had just dared to define their terms.

Aristotle

The beginning of wisdom is calling things by their right names.

Confucius

On July 26, 1945, the Potsdam Declaration urged Japan to surrender. Thereupon the Japanese Cabinet agreed that it was time to make peace, and on July 28 Premier Suzuki announced a policy of "mokosatsu." This unfortunate word has no exact counterpart in English. Its approximate meaning is "to withhold comment," but it also means "to ignore." The Domei News Agency at once broadcast in English that the Cabinet had decided to ignore the Potsdam ultimatum. After the atomic bombs had been dropped, President Truman cited the Japanese rejection of the ultimatum as a reason. Convincing evidence available since then shows that the Premier had indeed meant to convey "no comment," with the implication that a significant announcement would come later. Connoisseurs of the

Doctrine

ifs of history say that the right translation could have brought quick peace without atomic explosions.

Peter T. White

Joint and Service

A professional is one who does his best work when he feels the least like working.

Frank Lloyd Wright

It was not appreciated, and has scarcely been appreciated today, that the fighting power of an army is *the product and not the sum* of the arms composing it.

J. F. C. Fuller

The lesson from the last war that stands out clearly above all others is that if you want to go anywhere in modern war, in the air, on the sea, on the land, you must have command of the air.

Adm William F "Bull" Halsey
House Armed Services Committee report,
October 1949

We are about to invade the continent and have staked our success on our air superiority, on Soviet numerical preponderance, and on the high quality of our ground combat units.

GEN George C. Marshall
Memo to the Secretary of War, 1944

The use of military, naval and aerial forces in war should be directed toward a single end, to win. To attain maximum effectiveness these forces must be coordinated and in harmony with one another. The three forces should function as ingredients—or factors—of a single product in which the best results can be obtained only by a proper apportioning of the ingredients used.

Giulio Douhet

War is waged in three elements but there is no separate land, air, or naval war. Unless all assets in all elements are efficiently combined and coordinated against a . . . common objective, their maximum potential power cannot be realized.

Dwight Eisenhower

The point to understand is what the ultimate objective is, and instead of applying that objective to a land war and then organizing joint forces around the land war, let's look at it as we can apply military power directly to the objective.

Maj Gen Chuck Link, 1996

Now, I will be the first to admit that aerospace power let others down from the Peloponnesian through Spanish-American wars.

Gen Michael J. Dugan, USAF, retired, 1998

But I learned as a lieutenant that they were part-time soldiers, great when they were available, but not to be relied on routinely. They were never there at night, or in bad weather, or when "priorities" sent them elsewhere. . . . To my knowledge, it has not changed today, despite the additions of night vision, infrared sensors, and "smart" bombs. The Army has paid a high price for the unfulfilled promises of airpower since World War II—between wars in budget battles and during wars in facing enemy capabilities with

Doctrine

which we were unprepared to cope. . . . Even with the wondrous capabilities of today's technology, airpower is still a part-time participant.

GEN Frederick J. Kroesen

So long as large armies go to battle, so long will the air arm remain their spearhead.

Cyril Falls

The wider role of mobility and offensive power lies in the air. And the air force appears to be cast for the decisive role . . . in the future we need to think of the army and the air force as the two main components of military power.

B. H. Liddell Hart

You cannot beat an Air Force with an Army. You can't beat an Air Force with a Navy. But you can beat either of those with an Air Force. It has to do with physics.

Maj Gen Chuck Link

The US Army is incapable of surviving, much less prevailing, without overhead cover provided by the Air Force. It is myopic to think that money spent to control airspace somehow detracts from Army effectiveness. It makes Army effectiveness possible.

Loren B. Thompson

Joint warfare weaknesses of the U.S. Army, Navy, and Air Force:

Interservice rivalries limit coordination.
Intelligence does not reach operators rapidly.
Space satellites are vulnerable to direct attack.
Command control nodes are exposed to attack.
Ports and airfields are vulnerable in initial deployment.
Each high-tech weapon has its own weakness.
Aircraft carriers depend on E6 Prowlers.
U.S. forces are optimized for deserts, not mountains.

Li Zhiiyun, summarizing views of
75 PLA authors, 1995

We have good corporals and good sergeants and some good lieutenants and captains, and those are far more important than good generals.

GEN William Tecumseh Sherman

Doctrine

When I have young airmen who believe that an air power solution is the right thing to do but hesitate to say it for fear of appearing un-joint, it's going too far. If we create an environment in which we raise young military people to believe that it's okay to think one thing and say something else, than we'll be rotten at the core, and we can't afford that.

Maj Gen Chuck Link

Twenty Good Books

Arnold, Henry H. "Hap." *Report of the Commanding General of the Army Air Forces to the Secretary of War.* Washington, DC: War Department Bureau of Public Relations, 1944.

Borowski, Harry R., ed. *Harmon Memorial Lectures in Military History 1959–1987.* Washington, DC: Office of Air Force History, 1988.

Clausewitz, Carl von. *On War.* Translated by Anatol Rapoport. New York: Penguin Books, 1968.

Das, S. T. *An Introduction to the Art of War.* New Delhi: Sagar Publications, 1970.

de Seversky, Alexander P. *Victory through Air Power.* New York: Simon and Schuster, 1942.

Douhet, Giulio. *The Command of the Air.* Translated by Dino Ferrari. Washington, DC: Office of Air Force History, 1983.

Emme, Eugene M. *The Impact of Air Power: National Security and World Politics.* Princeton, NJ: D. Van Nostrand Co., Inc., 1959.

Fuller, J. F. C. *Generalship: Its Diseases and Their Cure.* Harrisburg, PA: Military Service Publishing Co., 1936.

Futrell, Robert F. *Ideas, Concepts, Doctrine: A History of Basic Thinking in the United States Air Force, 1907–1964.* Maxwell AFB, AL: Air University Press, 1971.

Heinl, Robert D., Jr. *Dictionary of Military and Naval Quotations.* Annapolis, MD: Naval Institute Press, 1966.

Kenney, George C. *General Kenney Reports.* Washington, DC: Office of Air Force History, 1987.

Liddell Hart, Basil H. *Strategy.* New York: New American Library, Inc., 1954.

Marshall, S. L. A. *The Officer as a Leader.* Harrisburg, PA: Stackpole Books, 1966.

Mitchell, William. *Skyways.* Philadelphia: J. B. Lippincott Co., 1930.

———. *Winged Defense.* Port Washington, NY: G. P. Putnam's Sons, 1925.

Paret, Peter, ed. *Makers of Modern Strategy: From Machcavelli to the Nuclear Age.* Princeton, NJ: Princeton University Press, 1986.

Sun Tzu. *The Art of War.* Translated by Samuel B. Griffith. New York: Oxford University Press, 1971.

Tedder, Arthur. *Air Power in War.* London: Hodder and Stoughton, 1948.

Warden, John A., III. *The Air Campaign.* Washington, DC: National Defense University Press, 1988.

Watts, Barry D. *The Foundations of U.S. Air Force Doctrine: The Problem of Friction in War.* Maxwell AFB, AL: Air University Press, 1984.

Source Index

Eccles, Henry E., 193–94
Echols, Oliver P., 14, 195
Einstein, Albert, 235
Eisenhower, Dwight D., 128, 168, 193, 243
Emerson, Ralph Waldo, 212
Emme, Eugene M., 24, 229
Enze, Shu, 136
Euripides, 197

Falls, Cyril, 244
Foch, Ferdinand, 6
Fogleman, Ronald R., 12, 20, 23, 32–33, 44, 109, 147–48,
    212
Fontenot, Gregory, 123
Forester, C. S., 183
Fortescue, John, 51
Frankland, Noble, 11
Franklin, Benjamin, 81, 189
Franz, Wallace P., 65
Frederick the Great, 3–4, 6, 51, 95, 171, 173, 189, 197, 206,
    212, 214
Frontinus, Sextus Julius, 56
Fuller, J. F. C., 7, 54, 65, 71, 76, 93, 137, 149, 162, 172,
    176–77, 191, 205, 218, 235, 237–38, 242
Fundamentals of British Maritime Doctrine, The, 44

Gabriel, Charles A., 191
Galland, Adolf, 46
Garstka, John, 135
Geiger, Keith W., 5
Genda, Minoru, 166
"General Air Force Principles," 165
Ghassan, 123
Global Reach–Global Power, 24
Goebbels, Joseph, 41
Gold, Philip, 22, 158
Gordon, Michael, 105
Grabowski, Thomas, 133
Greenfield, Meg, 84
Grimsley, William, 124
Groves, P. R. C., 30
Guderian, Heinz, 49
Guicciardini, Francesco, 85

Hackett, John W., 205
Hackworth, David, 104
Hagenbeck, Franklin L., 119
Hale, James O., 4

Odom, Thomas P., 104
Olds, Robin, 93, 176
O'Malley, Jerome F., 83
Oman, Sir Charles, 168
Omar, Mullah, 117
Orange, Vincent, 233
Ovid, 72
Owen, Robert C., 109, 110

Pace, Dave "Preacher," 3
Paine, Thomas, 66, 163
Palmer, Williston B., 211
Pape, Robert A., 108, 121
Patton, George S., 69, 169, 171, 212, 214
Patzalyuk, Viktor, 101
Pears, Sir Steuart, 87
Perry, William J., 132, 143
Peters, F. Whitten, 32, 137
Petrarch, 59
Pike, John, 124
Powell, Colin, 19, 115–16
Przybyslawski, Anthony F., 116
Pufeng, Wang, 135, 140
Puller, Lewis "Chesty," 213

Quanyou, Fu, 233
Quesada, Elwood R. "Pete," 223

Radford, Arthur, 17
Raleigh, Walter, 162
Ralston, Joe, 113
Reading, Rufus Isaacs, 85
Reimer, Dennis J., 109
Rezun, Miron, 102
Ridgway, Matthew B., 191
Roche, James G., 27
Rogers, F. M., 192
Rommel, Erwin, 46, 49, 53
Roosevelt, Theodore, 170
Roskill, S. W., 205
Ruge, Friedrich, 50
Rumsfeld, Donald, 116
Russell, Charles A., 86
Ryan, Michael, 33

Scales, Robert H., 104
Schriever, Bernard "Bernie," 28, 127
Schwarzkopf, Norman, 99, 215

Topical Index